William Ernest Henley

WILLIAM ERNEST HENLEY

A STUDY IN THE "COUNTER-DECADENCE"
OF THE 'NINETIES

BY JEROME HAMILTON BUCKLEY

PRINCETON UNIVERSITY PRESS · 1945
PRINCETON, NEW JERSEY

London: Humphrey Milford, Oxford University Press

TO MY MOTHER

The lyf so short, the craft so long to lerne,
Thassay so hard, so sharp the conquerynge,
The dredful joye, alwey that slit so yerne . . .

By some tacit agreement literary historians of the Victorian period have isolated a picturesque movement dominated by the hero-villain Oscar Wilde and known as the "decadence" of the "yellow 'nineties." The convenience of such a label has led many a reader virtually to ignore the truly vital writing of the English *fin de siècle*. For if there was in the 'nineties a "decadent" coterie, there was also a far more vigorous "counter-decadent" group. If there were the Wildean aesthetes, there were also the Young Men of William Ernest Henley. And it was in the theory and practice of the latter that the best in Edwardian letters was to take root.

This book attempts the first general criticism of Henley's life and work. Neither of the two biographers who have outlined his career has sought to evaluate his creative talent or to explain his profound influence on late Victorian literature. Leslie Cope Cornford has conjured up a semimythical literary giant; and Kennedy Williamson has sentimentalized a long struggle against debt and disease. In an effort to remedy the deficiency, I have deliberately slighted anecdote and personal melodrama, in order to relate Henley to a broader social, aesthetic, and intellectual background.

Apart from the many sources I have acknowledged in the progress of this study, I am deeply indebted to Mrs. Maude Henley and the Macmillan Company of London for permission to draw liberally upon Henley's original works; to Charles Scribner's Sons for American authorization to use the same material and for special permission to quote from the writings of Robert Louis Stevenson and from *The Colvins and Their Friends* by E. V. Lucas; to the Macmillan Company of New York for several passages from the *Autobiography* of William Butler Yeats; and to the Yale University Press for excerpts from C. Archer's monograph, *William Archer*. The frontispiece has been reproduced from Sir William

Rothenstein's admirable recollections, *Men and Memories*, by arrangement with the publishers, Faber and Faber, Ltd., London, and Coward-McCann, Inc., New York.

In the writing of this book, I have benefited immeasurably from the wise counsels of friends and colleagues. I appreciate the assistance of David Worcester, Franklin Newman, and James Keith Robinson in estimating the importance of Henley's verse, and the help of David Spring in interpreting the Victorian political complex. I am everlastingly grateful to my good wife, Elizabeth, not only for checking final proofs, but also for guiding me through innumerable decisions and revisions. And I am scarcely able to express my debt to Howard Mumford Jones, who has lent me constant encouragement and inspiration. In seeking a parallel to his enthusiasm for the subject in hand and to his forthright criticisms of my manuscript, I can revert only to "W. E. H." himself and the golden days of the *National Observer*.

J. H. B.

Madison, Wisconsin
November, 1944

CONTENTS

CONTENTS

ILLUSTRATIONS

William Ernest Henley

INTRODUCTION. CHAPTER 1. TOWARDS THE UNCONQUERABLE SOUL. THE VICTORIAN ACTIVIST PHILOSOPHIES

By virtue of a single poem William Ernest Henley remains at once the most freely quoted and the most thoroughly neglected of Victorian lyrists. All too frequently has "*Invictus*" been regarded as the sum total of its author's accomplishment. Protestant pastors have universally denounced its protesting agnosticism; while concert-hall baritones in every English-speaking community have tortured its heroics into rhythms wholly unsuited to its metrical design. In the judgment of the esoteric, its popular appeal has alone tended to detract from the poet's general reputation; for the taste of the common reader with whom Dr. Johnson once rejoiced to concur no longer serves as one of the scholar's criteria. Nevertheless, despite its truculency as an aesthetic unit, "*Invictus*" attains, when related to its proper context, all the emotional and intellectual impact of true poetry. It represents the logical culmination of a long struggle for life in the shadow of death. Its sources are profoundly personal; it arises literally "out of the night," out of the interminable hours of repose "lived on one's back," out of the invalid's desire to compensate his weakness in a "manly" lust for battle. Biographically, it marks, as we shall see, the turning point in an eventful career.

Yet the larger significance of "*Invictus*" far transcends any personal meaning. As a product of literature, it stems from an established literary tradition, a tradition which Professor Lowes has traced[1] back to the stoic fatalism of Beowulf and the defiance of the warriors at Maldon, caught in the clutch of circumstance. Enunciating an individual will to live, the poem is yet intelligible

---

[1] See John Livingston Lowes, *Convention and Revolt in Poetry* (Boston, 1919), ch. VIII, "The Anglo-Saxon Tradition."

only in the light of a faith which gave impetus to a whole golden age of individual achievement. Only in the perspective of an earlier philosophy of action[2] may we understand Henley's peculiar position in the late Victorian period. Only thus may we see his "activist" ethic in relation to the religion of the 'seventies, the art and drama of the 'eighties, the politics and poetry of the 'nineties.

IN the *Pall Mall Magazine* for August, 1900, Henley wrote with his usual self-assurance:

> On the whole, it looks as though Matthew Arnold had but grasped half the truth when he said that Byron and Wordsworth would head the procession of Nineteenth-Century English Poets into the "mist and hum" of the Twentieth Century. It may be Shelley and Byron; it may be Byron and Keats; it may be Byron and Coleridge. But, whoever the one, the other will certainly be Byron.

Later critics would probably agree that Arnold spoke only a half-truth; but few would find his judgment of Wordsworth erroneous. Most of them would repudiate Byron as the overpraised poet, Byron the ranting egoist, fundamentally insincere of thought and expression. None was readier than Henley to recognize the obvious; Byron he ranked even higher than the Italianate Rossetti as the arch-poseur of modern letters. But he was virtually alone in suggesting that the pose was a mere literary convention and that the man himself touched life with a humanity and realism unequaled since the time of Shakespeare. To be sure, he admitted, *The Giaour* rang hollow in its false sentiments; but was not, he asked, the Giaour "preferable, man for man, before the hero of *Jenny*?" Against the factitious remorse of

[2] The survey of Victorian "activism" which follows is intended to be representative rather than exhaustive. Authors have been selected for citation by reason of their popular vogue as well as their literary significance; and where possible, Henley's attitude towards his "activist" predecessors has been indicated.

4

the mawkish mid-Victorian profligate, he could place
the brave confession of a hero who had lived danger-
ously, desperately, abundantly. Byron was himself the
Giaour; and with all "the excellence of sincerity and
strength," he proclaimed through his character's lips
the high adventure of active living:

> I've 'scaped the weariness of Life:
> Now leagued with friends, now girt by foes,
> I loathed the languor of repose.
> Now nothing left to love or hate,
> No more with hope or pride elate,
> I'd rather be the thing that crawls
> Most noxious o'er a dungeon's walls,
> Than pass my dull, unvarying days
> Condemned to meditate and gaze.

As a statement of activism, these lines were not less
clear than Stevenson's admonition to the monks of Our
Lady of the Snows. Henley refused to assume behind
them a spurious emotion; he knew from personal experience the necessity of self-assertion. If he were to
indicate the melodramatic element in *The Giaour*, the
element of attitudinizing "Byronism," he might have
pointed to its conclusion, where a conventional *Welt-
schmerz*, a weary yearning for nirvana, displaced the
virile philosophy:

> Despair is stronger than the will.
> Waste not thine orison, despair
> Is mightier than thy pious prayer:
> I could not, if I might, be blest;
> I want no Paradise, but rest.

But to Henley, Byron was simply the greatest of English
activists; he was the supreme satirist, the lover of pugilism, the soldier of Missolonghi; he was master of a difficult craft, skilled in all the arts of vigorous self-expression; he was the creator of a literature and a legend.
And Henley's was by no means a wholly unsound
interpretation of an extroverted and versatile gentleman
under the Regency. But to the greater part of the nine-

5

teenth century, Byron's legend was stronger than Byron's personality; the melancholy Childe Harold and "the pageant of his bleeding heart" were realities far more apparent than the robust earthiness of the author of *Don Juan*. In consequence, the Victorian ethic of action was rather a revolt against Byronic negation than an outgrowth of Byronic individualism.

Thomas Carlyle was foremost in point of time and of vehemence among major Victorian prophets; for fifty years he poured forth such torrents of sense and nonsense as even the most phlegmatic could not ignore. Indeed, from one point of view, the whole Victorian era may be said to begin with the stern commandment that rings through the calculated hocus-pocus of *Sartor Resartus*, "Close thy Byron, open thy Goethe." It was not that the Victorians obeyed; for *The Pilgrimage* and "The Prisoner of Chillon" seldom lay shut in drawing rooms and private libraries which would have been fiercely defended against the entrance of the poet; and for the few that opened *Faust*, many more found an admirable substitute in Philip Bailey's *Festus*. Nevertheless, Carlyle's effect was far from negligible. If Byron was still read, he was no longer read seriously; his rhetoric was more audible than Shelley's music and, therefore, more moving; but the vogue of the Byronic dandy, including Pelham and Disraeli's Duke of St. James, had already passed, and Manfred screaming curses from a mountain top seemed a trifle ridiculous. On the other hand, if the true Goethe received but little attention, the Goethe of Carlyle's imagining came to be regarded as the incarnation of righteous energy.[3] He joined hands with the Hebraists—the Wesleyan, the Calvinist, the Evangelical of Clapham—to lend moral support to a Benthamite philosophy of work. Without his example,

[3] George Henry Lewes's thoughtful interpretation of Goethe the artist and scientist made no specific repudiation of Carlyle's vision of Goethe the moralist.

6

Victorian activism would have lacked its most vital inspiration.

Carlyle's enthusiasm for Goethe rested on a basic misconception. He confused the serenity of a disinterested artist with the detachment of a philosopher engrossed by ontological values. From the outset he pictured Goethe as a transcendentalist in communion with the World Soul:

> Knowest thou no Prophet, even in the vesture, environment, and dialect of this age? None to whom the Godlike had revealed itself, through all the meanest and highest forms of the Common; and by him been again prophetically revealed: in whose inspired melody even in these rag-gathering and rag-burning days, Man's Life again begins, were it but afar off, to be divine? Knowest thou none such? I know him, and name him—Goethe.

Thus it was Goethe the moral teacher, the prophet of the ultimates, to whom Carlyle paid homage. It mattered not that this teacher consistently distrusted all forms of mysticism; he yet served as prototype for the troubled metaphysician of *Sartor* who must needs, "over the whole surface of the earth (by footprints), write his *Sorrows of Teufelsdröckh*; even as the great Goethe, in passionate words, had to write his *Sorrows of Werter*, before the spirit freed herself, and he could become a Man." At a crucial stage in his emotional development, Carlyle had come upon a Man, whose "serenity, breadth, and tolerance, achieved after heroic struggle, gave significance to his own problems."[4] "Your works," he wrote to the master, "have been a mirror to me; unasked and unhoped-for, your wisdom has counselled me; and so peace and health of soul have visited me from afar."[5] Goethe, he could read in his own terms; the transition from *Werther* to *Meister* paralleled the passing from the Everlasting No to the Everlasting Yea: "We found

[4] Charles Frederick Harrold, *Carlyle and German Thought* (New Haven, 1934), p. 11.

[5] Charles Eliot Norton, ed., *Correspondence between Goethe and Carlyle* (London, 1887), p. 34.

7

him in darkness and now he is in light; . . anarchy has now become peace."

In this great original intellect converting anarchy into peace, shaping order out of chaos, Carlyle found a symbol of the domination of mind over matter, of the Clothes-Philosophy in action. The achievement of the Abbot Samson confuted the indolence of Byronism; it pointed the moral of Goethe's chorus:

> Heard are the Voices,
> Heard are the Sages,
> The Worlds and the Ages:
> "Choose well; your choice is
> Brief and yet endless.
>
> Here eyes do regard you,
> In Eternity's stillness;
> Here is all fulness,
> Ye brave, to reward you;
> Work and despair not."

Tirelessly Carlyle sounded the same note again and again; drawing what he would from the German poet, he provided his generation with a gospel of labor:

Work is of a religious nature:—work is of a *brave* nature; which it is the aim of all religion to be. All work of man is as the swimmer's: a waste ocean threatens to devour him; if he front it not bravely, it will keep its word. By incessant wise defiance of it, lusty rebuke and buffet of it, behold how it loyally supports him, bears him as its conqueror along. "It is so," says Goethe, "with all things that man undertakes in this world."

Goethe became the first of the Carlylean heroes; Goethe served as proof that all creative effort is good, "all work . . . is noble; work is alone noble."

Sartor and *Past and Present* introduced Goethe to the Victorian public as an apostle of the active life. And to a degree, this was a valid presentation of an author whose masterpiece embodied the idea that existence was coterminous with aspiration and that death de-

8

scended upon the human being as soon as he could say
contentedly unto the moment, "*Verweile doch, du bist
so schön!*" The essential difference between Carlyle's
prophetic hero and the author of *Faust* was not the opposition of denial and assent; for both were prepared to
accept life in its fullness. It was rather a difference in
the sanctions that underlay two assertive philosophies.
According to Carlyle, Goethe taught that it was man's
function, his moral obligation, to serve as an active agent
of the Creative Principle in the universe. It is unlikely
that the real Goethe ever for long entertained any such
notion. For Goethe was primarily the artist rather than
the moralist; and his search for self-realization was aesthetic rather than ethical in origin and direction. John
Stuart Mill, who saw the matter more clearly than
Carlyle, denied a higher than personal significance to
Goethe's morality; the poet's writings were, he said,
"penetrated throughout by views of morals and of conduct in life, often in my opinion not defensible, but
which are incessantly seeking whatever defence they
admit of in the theory of the right and duty of self-
development."[6] By implication, this criticism traces Goe-
thean assertion to the demands of the individual will
rather than to any universal moral sense. In so doing, it
suggests the basis of late Victorian activism; Henley
and Stevenson were forever conscious not of a social
morality but of "the right and duty of self-development."
Yet to the 'fifties and 'sixties, the ethical sanction proffered by Carlyle furnished by far the most stringent
postulate for a code of action and industry.[7]

Tennyson's eyes filled with tears as he entered the
low-ceilinged room at Weimar that had been Goethe's

[6] John Stuart Mill, *Autobiography* (London, 1924), p. 217.
[7] In his essay on Heine, Arnold, who interpreted Goethe as the
Hellenist rather than the Hebraist, acknowledged Carlyle's importance
as the German's most voluble advocate. Later J. R. Seeley wrote: "We
cannot help reflecting . . . how much his reputation among ourselves
has been the work of Mr. Carlyle."—Seeley, *Goethe after Sixty Years*
(Boston, 1893), p. 163.

9

study.[8] It was fitting that he above all others should pay tribute at the prophet's shrine. For he was Laureate of England in the fullest sense of the word; he typified what was best in the solid middle class. Born a craftsman, he had made himself a poet; he had withdrawn from a Palace of Art to share in the turmoil of a troubled age. The Victorians hearkened unto him; for he spoke with angel's tongue of their common hopes and fears and ideals. In his period of apprenticeship, he had written two poems expressing with singular felicity the two moods that were to struggle for ascendancy in the art and life of the entire century. "The Lotos-Eaters" is full of sleep and weariness, a sad sweet symphony of death and defeat and resignation; in it is all of an artist's yearning for escape, his passionate desire to forget this rotten world:

> Let us swear an oath, and keep it with an equal mind,
> In the hollow Lotos-land to live and lie reclined
> On the hills like gods together, careless of mankind.

Its companion piece sounds a clarion call to the unconquerable soul, a summons to

> heroic hearts
> Made weak by time and fate but strong in will
> To strive, to seek, to find, and not to yield.

"Ulysses" is a paean to the active life that loathes "the languor of repose":

> How dull it is to pause, to make an end,
> To rust unburnished, not to shine in use,
> As though to breathe were life!

Each poem captures a recurrent state of mind; each is a brilliant exercise in form and movement; neither, I think, was intended as a statement of personal faith. "The Lotos-Eaters" carries the sensuous strain in English verse from Keats to the Pre-Raphaelites; and in its hedonism it foreshadows the *Rubáiyàt* and the poetry of "decadence." "Ulysses," on the other hand, forms a link

[8] See J.-M. Carré, *Goethe en Angleterre* (Paris, 1920), p. 259.

in the literature of will between Byron and Henley. And
"Ulysses," originally conceived as an objective, dramatic monologue, represents Tennyson's own final philosophy. When the poet had outgrown his experimental
period and had passed through the doubt and sentimentality of his middle years,[9] he turned as an old man
from the sickly aesthetes he had influenced, to a last
analysis of the conflicts that had rocked his generation.
At the age of eighty, he wrote "Vastness," a courageous
summing-up of the long intellectual and emotional
struggle, in which, as Henley said, "the insight into
essentials, the command of primordial matter, the capacity of vital suggestion, are gloriously in evidence
from the first line to the last."[10] In "Vastness" Tennyson
stripped his verse of ornament and sweetness: he stood
like his own oak tree,

> All his leaves
>   Fall'n at length,
> Look, he stands,
>   Trunk and bough,
>   Naked strength.

At the end of his life he could look back without regret;
he could sing the challenge to heroic hearts:

> O young Mariner,
> Down to the haven,
> Call your companions,
> Launch your vessel,
> And crowd your canvas,
> And ere it vanishes
> Over the margin,
> After it, follow it,
> Follow the Gleam.

This was the Tennyson that Henley admired and that
subsequent critics have tended to neglect. Yet even in

[9] In his late poetry Tennyson writes with a new freedom from constraint. The vivid harlot image of "Romney's Remorse," for instance,
could scarcely be matched in the verse of the earlier volumes.

[10] *The Works of William Ernest Henley*, 5 vols. (London, 1921),
IV, 142.

Maud and the *Idylls,* this masculine strain was never in complete abeyance. For all his Lady Clara Vere de Veres, his May Queens, his Annie Lees, the mid-Victorians found Tennyson consistent in his "manliness," strong in his will to live the full life according to the dictates of God and conscience.

A moral activism comparable to that of Tennyson supplies the *leitmotif* of much good and bad nineteenth century verse, whether or not such verse owes any conceivable debt to the preachings of the Laureate. It was present until the end in the optimism of Robert Browning, from the resolute "Childe Roland" to the gallant "Epilogue" which declares lifelong devotion to the manly virtues:

> What had I on earth to do
> With the slothful, with the mawkish, the unmanly?
> Like the aimless, helpless, hopeless, did I drivel
> —Being—who?

It was an element in the stoic defiance of Matthew Arnold:

> Charge once more, and then be dumb;
> Let the victors when they come,
> When the forts of folly fall,
> Find thy body by the wall.

And whatever the source of her inspiration, the philosophy made its impress on Adelaide Anne Procter. Man, she wrote, must forever fight valiantly in the cause of truth; no sinful sloth may purchase his security:

> The greater peril in the strife,
> The less this evil should be done;
> For as in battle, so in life,
> Danger and honor still are one.

Nor must the hero seek alone the glory of conquest; duty demands that he awaken his sluggard brother to the call of the battle:

> Arouse him then:—this is thy part:
> Show him the claim; point out the need;

12

And nerve his arm, and cheer his heart;
Then stand aside, and say, "God speed!"

The same morality runs through the nine hundred editions of *Proverbial Philosophy*.[11] It was Martin Tupper's profound conviction that there could be no rest on earth or in heaven, that a longing for Lotus-land was immoral, that the soul could realize itself only in active living:

Seekest thou rest, O mortal?—seek it no more on earth,
For destiny will not cease from dragging thee through
    the rough wilderness of life;
Seekest thou rest, O immortal?—hope not to find it in
    Heaven,
For sloth yieldeth not happiness: the bliss of a spirit is
    action.

In so repudiating "rest," Tupper felt it necessary to explain through a learned gloss that he had no quarrel with the New Testament connotation of that word; he objected rather to the romantic interpretation of the term, specifically to the Byronic usage, for the slothful rest that the weary Giaour covets "is not possible, or is at any rate very improbable, in the case of spiritual creatures." Tupper thus obeyed at least the first half of Carlyle's command; he closed his Byron as unchristian and unmanly.

The poets of moral activism encouraged a mood inherent in the very nature of a widening democracy. Newly enfranchised, the middle classes aggressively accepted the social order that had made possible their rise to power. Upon the Captains of Industry the future of England depended; and Carlyle set out to awaken heroism in their capitalistic souls. But the bourgeois philosophy proved pragmatic rather than transcendental. Assertion became an economic necessity as well as a spiritual duty. In less than a generation, the Philistine complex had established a prerogative. Its ideals had been implicit in Macaulay's *History*. They were at

[11] See Clement Shorter, *Victorian Literature* (New York, 1897), p. 27.

once vulgarized and canonized by the facile pen of Samuel Smiles, whose *Self-help; with Illustrations of Character, Conduct, and Perseverance* proved beyond doubt that honesty was the only policy. Nor did the Philistine confine these ideals to the Herculean labors he had undertaken. He carried his enthusiasms into the shrinking world of the Barbarian. The amiable Mr. Jorrocks, as early as 1831, had bridged the gulf between the tradesman and the fox-hunting squire. And in the years that followed, the Englishman's appetite for action was far from sated by the tremendous advance of the mercantile system; Miss Thorne of Ullathorne had really no cause to worry about the degeneracy of British youth. By the early 'seventies, W. G. Grace with his cricket bat commanded more respect than W. E. Gladstone with his domestic reforms. In their love of sport as in their love of work, the Victorians were tense, eager, earnest. They could understand the impulse behind the suicide pact of *Red Pottage*, by which a character "is pledged to leave this world within four months, or shall we say five, on account of the pheasant shooting?" Taken by and large, they were all determined activists; they were blind to the "isms" and the "ologies" that were leading artists and intellectuals to question the worth and purpose of living.

On their less materialistic side, Victorian middle-class virtues derived freely from the standards of the English public schools, which, in turn, were revitalized by bourgeois wealth and energy. The earliest of the great headmasters, Dr. Arnold of Rugby, fostered the cult of "manliness." And his principles colored the whole generation's activist philosophy. The adjective "manly" came to signify general approval; while "unmanly" served as a favorite opprobrious epithet. Though Thackeray complained in his well-known preface to *Pendennis* that "since the author of 'Tom Jones' was buried, no writer of fiction among us has been permitted to depict to his utmost power a Man," he could nonetheless describe the fully depicted Colonel Newcome as "a fine manly-looking fellow."[12] There was no obvious contradiction between the novelist's theory and his practice; for "manly" and "masculine" were scarcely assumed to be synonymous terms. A judgment of "manliness" had essentially moral rather than physical implications. Guy Morville, the heir of Redclyffe, became the ideal hero of the 'fifties not because he risked death to rescue a boatload of drowning fishermen, not because he braved the elements to snatch his beloved Amy from the brink of an Alpine gorge, but rather because he endured with Christian forbearance the envy and malice of Cousin Philip. His manliness lay in his health of soul. Similarly, Sir Galahad's strength was as the strength of ten, *because* his heart was pure. And John Ridd's courage mounted from a sense of moral rectitude as he grappled with Carver Doone by the black bog of Exmoor. Without godliness there had been no manliness. Brawn without brain, body without soul, this was the mark of the brute or the coward. Wilkie Collins in 1870 wrote *Man and Wife* to show the bestiality of a mere athlete towards a sensitive woman. Twelve years later, Bernard Shaw set out to prove through *Cashel Byron's Profession* that a moronic Adonis was biologically well suited to his intellectual spouse. The difference between the two novels is significant; for it indicates a difference in approach to the problems of human conduct. By the 'eighties "manliness" which implied certain inhibitions was no longer the cardinal virtue. In the jargon of a new science, a capacity for survival seemed more relevant than moral fervor to the desire for a life of action.

Integral to many philosophies of the mid-Victorian period, the ideals of activism received their strongest and fullest literary expression in the writings of George Borrow and of Charles and Henry Kingsley. Borrow was

---

[12] This is actually the remark of Smith, "the cock of the school," but it is obviously also the novelist's view.

not truly representative of his time; and Henley wrote of him as of a visitant from another world:

> Three hundred years since Borrow would have been a gentleman adventurer: he would have dropped quietly down the river, and steered for the Spanish Main, bent upon making carbonadoes of your Don. But he came too late for that, and falling upon no sword and buckler age but one that was interested in Randal and Spring, he accepted that he found, and did his best to turn its conditions into literature. As he had that admirable instinct of making the best of things which marks the true adventurer, he was on the whole exceeding happy.[13]

Borrow's happiness inspires the most lyrical passage in that strange picaresque medley of pugilism and pedantry called *Lavengro*. The dialogue between the scholar-gipsy and the Romany Chal is perhaps too familiar to merit quotation; yet no summary of activist tendencies, however brief, could afford to pass it by. Jasper reminds Lavengro of the joy of living:

> "Life is sweet, brother."
> "Do you think so?"
> "Think so! There's night and day, brother, both sweet things; sun, moon, and stars, brother, all sweet things; there's likewise the wind on the heath. Life is very sweet, brother; who would wish to die—"
> "I would wish to die—"
> "You talk like a gorgio—which is the same as talking like a fool—were you a Romany Chal you would talk wiser. Wish to die, indeed! A Romany Chal would wish to live forever!"
> "In sickness, Jasper?"
> "There's the sun and stars, brother."
> "In blindness, Jasper?"
> "There's the wind on the heath, brother; if I could only feel that I would gladly live forever. Dosta, we'll now go to the tents and put on the gloves; and I'll try to make you feel what a sweet thing it is to be alive, brother!"

[13] *Works*, IV, 121.

Such easy acceptance of things as they are stands at a long remove from the furious assertion of Carlyle or the deliberate assent of Stevenson. Without a metaphysic to be realized, without a disease to be compensated, Jasper is content to live forever in his tents on the heath; his delight in natural phenomena is spontaneous; he seeks not its cause, nor questions its result. It was quite another matter with the Kingsleys. The muscular Christians could have had little sympathy with Borrow and his carefree companions of the road.

Henry Kingsley, whom Henley deemed a more gifted writer than Charles,[14] lacked Borrow's ability to find romance in the green fields of England. He dreamed of action more purposeful than the fox hunting that delighted Mr. Jorrocks. He asked virtues more heroic than the pragmatism of Samuel Smiles and the Manchester School. Expelled from Oxford, he sought adventure in the Australian wilderness. And he turned his varied experience to good account in the melodramatic *Recollections of Geoffry Hamlin*. His best novel, *Ravenshoe*, apart from its puerile polemic against Roman Catholicism, is remarkable for its protest against the busyness of the Philistine and the ennui of the Barbarian. Defrauded by a scheming priest of his Irish estates and brought by circumstance to menial labor, the hero refuses to acknowledge personal defeat; from his degraded post as groomsman, he rises to answer the challenge of battle. En route to the war in Crimea, he recovers his own peace of mind:

> The lowest menial drudgery was exalted and glorified. Groom his horse and help clean the deck? Why not? That horse must carry him in the day of the merry meeting of heroes. Hard living, hard work, bad weather, disease, death: what were they, with his youth, strength, and nerve? Not to be thought of save with a smile.

As the young master of Ravenshoe regains his assent in

---

[14] See Leslie Cope Cornford, *William Ernest Henley* (London, 1913), p. 10.

17

devotion to a cause, so Henry Kingsley identified himself with the larger issues of his time. The first Englishman to enter fallen Sedan in the fateful September of
1870, he strove to awaken his countrymen to the tragedy
of Western Europe. Foreign correspondent, novelist,
explorer, idealist, he found his individuality in arduous
altruism.

No less an activist than his brother, Charles Kingsley
passed his strenuous life in preaching to the Victorians
rather than in rebelling against their standards. He wrote
articles, editorials, tracts, pamphlets, letters, novels,
poems, sermons, designed to propagate the ideals of
"Christian Socialism." He translated the message of
Carlyle into evangelical terms; he applied the philosophy of work towards the immediate physical and spiritual betterment of the workers involved. He labored long
in the cause of reform. Yet he was almost as firm a be-
liever in tradition as Father Newman whom he attacked;
and he spent a considerable part of his fifty-six years in
reminding his fellow Britons of their cultural heritage.
Among the novels, *Two Years Ago* will serve perhaps
best to illustrate the principles of action that underlay
his manifold effort. The hero of the fiction, Tom Thurnall, has alone survived shipwreck off the coast of Devon,
largely through the efforts of Grace Harvey who led a
group of peasants to the rescue. In their first conversation, Tom alarms Grace by the "Stoic optimism" with
which he counters her Christian humility:

"All taken and you alone left! God must have high
things in store for you. He must have a great work for
you to do. Else, why are you not as one of these? O,
think! where would you have been at this moment if
God had dealt with you as with them?"

"Where I am now, I suppose," said Tom, quietly.

"Where you are now?"

"Yes, where I ought to be. I am where I ought to be
now. I suppose, if I had found myself anywhere else
this morning, I should have taken it as a sign that I was
wanted there, and not here."

18

Grace heaved a sigh at words which were certainly startling. The Stoic optimism of the world-hardened doctor was new and frightful to her.

Tom has the virtue of candor; but he has yet to learn that honest Stoicism is insufficient faith to bear him through the reverses of an active life. His redemption, like that of Charles in *Ravenshoe*, is bought by hard experience in the Crimean War. Returning home after eighteen months in a Russian prison, he tells Grace how "a boorish villain of a khan" stopped him short in an ambitious career; but Grace interrupts his narrative:

"He did not stop you; God stopped you!"

"You're right, Grace; I saw that at last! I found out that I had been trying for years which was the stronger, God or I; I found out I had been trying whether I could not do well enough without Him; and there I found that I could not, Grace;—could not! I felt like a child who had marched off from home, fancying it can find its way, and is lost at once. . . . I did not know that I had a Father in heaven, who had been looking after me, when I fancied that I was looking after myself. . . . Teach me, Grace!"

In the light of such humility, Tom is virtually transfigured; Grace eagerly accepts his proffered love:

She leapt up at him suddenly, as if waking from a dream, and wreathed her arms about his neck.

"O, Mr. Thurnall! my dear, brave, wise, wonderful Mr. Thurnall! come home again!—home to God! and home to me! I am not worthy! Too much happiness, too much,—too much. . . ."

And so the old heart passed away from Thomas Thurnall; and instead of it grew up a heart like his father's; even the heart of a little child.

The moral of the novel is pointed beyond mistake: however strong man's particular will, his whole power lies in his dependence upon the universal Will; self-assertion has meaning only when the self acts humbly in accordance with the laws of God and nature.

Kingsley returned again and again to this central problem, the relation of the individual to the Universal. A year before his death, he published his *Westminster Sermons*, one of which attempted to clarify the apparent contradiction between an egotistical desire to achieve personality and a willingness to subserve the divine purpose. At the outset, the sermon declares that the personal element in human life is God-given and indestructible, and that there is no escape from the realities of conscience and consciousness:

> How many people, in this Christian land, are saying at this very moment to themselves, "Oh, that I could get rid of this I myself in me, which is so discontented and unhappy! Oh, that I could forget myself!" . . . It is all in vain. There is no escape from self.

Yet the clutch of circumstance is not so fell that the unconquerable soul cannot shake itself free:

> For what rises in [men], or seems to rise, more and more painfully and fiercely? What but that protest, that battle, between the everlasting I within them, and their own passions, and motives, and circumstances?

Thus the vigorous soul instinctively finds fulfillment in assertion; it needs no call to action. Yet if it is to accomplish a positive work, it must be governed by godly impulse:

> Some here, surely, have read Epictetus, the heathen whose thought most exactly coincides with that of the Psalmist. If so, do they not see what enabled him, the slave of Nero's minion, to *assert himself, and his own unconquerable personality; to defy circumstance*; and to preserve his own calm, his own honour, his own purity, amid a degradation which might well have driven a good man to suicide? And was it not this— The intensity of his faith in God? In God the helper, God the guide?[15]

In phrasing, this passage anticipates "*Invictus*," written

---

[15] *Westminster Sermons* (London, 1874), pp. 167, 170, 173, italics mine.

in the following year. But though it speaks of indomitable will and defiance of fate, it endows the truly heroic individual with implicit trust in a divine Benevolence. "*Invictus*" rests on no such faith; the poet stands alone, a defiant agnostic, exultant in his strong free will, whatever gods may be.

To a skeptical younger generation, Kingsley's sermon must have seemed quite irrelevant. It was vain to expound the theological sanctions of activism at a time when all theological values were subject to question; a dying religion could not quicken a lust for life. Already, by the 'seventies, the vitality of a Protestant faith had passed. Winwood Reade had written scornfully of the hollow half-gods: "Supernatural Christianity is false. God-worship is idolatry. Prayer is useless. The soul is not immortal. There are no rewards and punishments in a future state."[16] But if the half-gods had gone, the gods themselves were slow in arriving. Arnold, who wished to preserve something of a tradition to which he could not subscribe, spoke vaguely of "the power not ourselves that makes for righteousness." Yet this belief in a force for good proved as untenable intellectually as the dogmatism it sought to replace; and it lacked utterly the emotional drive of Christian theism. Arnold's nebulosity was, however, characteristic of all such intellectuals as felt a nostalgia for the old religion. In his notebook, Benjamin Jowett commented on the similar credo of his friend, T. H. Green:

> G. wants to write a sermon in which the language of theology is omitted—a Christian discourse meaning the same thing in other words.
>
> The attempt is worth making, but it requires great genius to execute it. The words will seem thin, moral, unitarian. . . . Those who give up orthodoxy have nothing to support them; they have no words responding to their higher thoughts. They bury themselves in the physical world, or are lost in systems or abstractions.

[16] *The Martyrdom of Man* (10th ed., London, 1885), p. 523.

21

"I will put a new heart in you, not like the former heart," seems too much for any mortal to say.[17]

The contributors to *Essays and Reviews*—and Jowett among them—who had attempted to reconcile Anglicanism to science, had succeeded only in undermining the structure of orthodoxy. They suffered not less than the faithful whom they had confounded; they lost the strongest incentive to living; and no new prophet arose to enspirit them.[18]

The Religion of Humanity was the most specious of the substitutes for theism; but it proved no more satisfying to its adherents than any other ethical philosophy that dispensed with a supernatural absolute. In his last essay, Mill, the greatest of the English Comtists, groped pathetically for the faith that he had never known; with mental courage and emotional timidity, he strained to imagine, as the postulate of moral conduct, a good God of circumscribed power.

Swinburne felt a profound contempt for John Morley and the *Fortnightly* positivists who attacked his verses. Yet he was deeply impregnated with the doctrines of the Party of Humanity; and under the influence of its principles, he wrote his most serious poetry. The "Prelude" to *Songs before Sunrise* proclaims man's independence of things supernatural; the rational soul seeks inspiration not from myth but from the realities of a sensuous world:

> For what has he whose will sees clear
> To do with doubt and faith and fear,
>   Swift hopes and slow despondencies?
>   His heart is equal with the sea's
> And with the sea-wind's, and his ear
>   Is level to the speech of these,

[17] Quoted by Evelyn Abbott and Lewis Campbell, *The Life and Letters of Benjamin Jowett, M.A.*, 2 vols. (London, 1897), II, 77. *Cf.* the sermon delivered in Mallock's *New Republic*, 1877.

[18] In the 'eighties social service work and imperialist politics became common substitutes for religion; *cf. All Sorts and Conditions of Men* (1882) and *Robert Elsmere* (1888), and see below, pp. 134-35.

And his soul communes and takes cheer
  With the actual earth's equalities,
Air, light, and night, hills, winds, and streams
And seeks not strength from strengthless dreams.

Continuing on its wordy way, the poem reaches its climax in the metaphor of the ship at sea:

Because man's soul is man's God still,
What wind soever waft his will
    Across the waves of day and night,
    To port or shipwreck, left or right,
By shores and shoals of good and ill;
    And still its flame at mainmast height
Through the rent air that foam-flakes fill
    Sustains the indomitable light
Whence only man hath strength to steer
Or helm to handle without fear.

This stanza bears a superficial resemblance to the much condensed last line of "*Invictus.*" But the resemblance ceases when we disentangle a meaning from the Swinburnean verbiage. Man is not the captain of the soul; he is hardly even its cabin boy; the individual will goes with the wind, and only the soul is steadfast in its purpose. What then, we ask, does the poet understand by the "soul"? But this he fails to make clear. In a salute to Walt Whitman, "soul" seems equivalent to the spirit of Freedom abroad in the universe. In the "Prelude," it appears to mean nothing more definite than the vague life-force that animates a physical being; it appears to be merely a deliberate agnostic's euphemism for God the Creator. And in "Hertha," it is more definitely the spirit of Earth, the divine nisus, surging ever upward through a timeless evolution. But nowhere in Swinburne does soul ever become, as in Kingsley's sermon, the basis of human personality. Consequently, despite a lyric cry for Liberty, there is nowhere a sense of individual worth. And without faith in the survival of the self, there is no deep yearning for the full experience.

23

If Swinburne outgrew the studied indolence of *Poems and Ballads,* he never for long ceased thanking

> Whatever gods may be
> That no life lives forever;
> That dead men rise up never;
> That even the weariest river
> Winds somewhere safe to sea.

Throughout his work, the passionate wooing of sleep and death recurs more frequently than the eager desire for wakeful life. Though "The Garden of Proserpine" is the obvious source of Henley's "Whatever gods may be," it is as far removed from *"Invictus"* as the Everlasting No from the Everlasting Yea. For all his later imperialism and his altruistic concern with larger causes, Swinburne never, insofar as the individual soul was concerned, passed beyond the Centre of Indifference. Without faith in the personal entity, he was unable to formulate a genuine activist philosophy.

Swinburne's longing to escape from the tyranny of self-consciousness was symptomatic of a general late Victorian lassitude. From a long civil war between the Knowable and the Unknowable, the best of English intellects were weary; no longer could the partisans of either faction be greatly excited by ultimate victory or defeat. In his Dublin address to the British Association for the Advancement of Science, Professor Tyndall decried the mental exhaustion of the age, and strove to reawaken its dormant enthusiasm:

> It is perfectly possible for you and me to purchase intellectual peace at the price of intellectual death. . . . I would exhort you . . . to scorn base repose—to accept, if the choice be forced upon you, commotion before stagnation, the leap of the torrent before the stillness of the swamp. In the one there is at all events life, and therefore, hope; in the other none.

But the 'seventies as a whole were less earnest than John Tyndall; they were better able to appreciate the absurdity of Mallock's Mr. Stockton than the high seriousness of the lecturer-scientist. For the average cultivated reader was losing interest in metaphysical disputation. In 1869 he welcomed *The Earthly Paradise* as an antidote[19] to *The Ring and the Book* and the *New Poems* of Matthew Arnold, and so established Morris's reputation as an "escapist" poet. While he had been thoroughly shaken by *The Origin of Species* in 1859, he received Darwin's far more explicit *Descent of Man* in 1871 with comparative calm; and he had so far forgotten the religious conflict by 1882 that he buried the evolutionist with due Anglican ritual in the crypt of Westminster Abbey. Whereas the early Victorian had considered the decay of dogma a threat to his moral, mental, and even physical stability, the late Victorian found that, by a few psychological adjustments, he might continue to live quite comfortably without the support of religion. We may gauge this decline of spirituality by a comparison of James Anthony Froude's *Nemesis of Faith* (1849) with William Hale White's *Autobiography of Mark Rutherford* (1881). Each book treats of a young clergyman whose doubt has led him to renounce the tenets of orthodoxy. Driven by remorse into the Roman Church, Markham Sutherland of the earlier novel perishes in utter disillusion:

> He was infected with the plague. Earth was lost to him. Heaven was a dreary blank. One by one, as he had wandered in the wilderness of speculation, the beacon lights of life had gone out, or sunk below the horizon.

Mark Rutherford is more fortunate; he survives the night of despair to rejoice in the new dawn:

> As I got older I became aware of the folly of this perpetual reaching after the future, and of drawing from to-morrow, and from to-morrow only, a reason for the joyfulness of to-day. I learned, when alas! it was almost too late, to live each moment as it passed over my head,

---

[19] See Oscar Maurer, Jr., "William Morris and the Poetry of Escape," Herbert Davis, ed., *Nineteenth-Century Studies* (Ithaca, N.Y., 1940), p. 266.

believing that the sun as it is now rising is as good as it ever will be, and blinding myself as much as possible to what may follow.

Whether or not such withdrawal from the conflict meant that intellectual peace had been purchased at the price of intellectual death was of small concern to a generation weary of the battle. Mark Rutherford's fatalistic hedonism was the only practicable substitute for the vanished theology; it was the inevitable outgrowth of an enervating struggle.

Less than a year after James Thomson had branded London the City of Dreadful Night, Henley was carried exultant from the Royal Infirmary out into the April sunshine and the joyous bustle of an Edinburgh morning. He was free in the great, the "wonderful" world; and "all his nature sprang up to hail the divinity of life."[20] Always he would hear the helpless, hopeless Thomson's "dirge on a xylophone" with utter disdain; and one day he would roar out against "B. V.'s" blasphemy: "The Freethinker thinks he is confuting Christ, when he is only chaffing the parish beadle."[21] Essentially, *"Invictus"* was an inversion of Victorian defeatism into terms of a personal assent. It proclaimed the militant optimist, the soul unconquerable whatever gods might be, the rebel strong in his revolt against death and denial.

On the publication of Henley's first poems, George Meredith wrote to the poet that "the rude realism" of the hospital verses had "braced" him,—"and with this breath of the darkness of life you give a note—'Out of the night that covers me'—which has a manful ring to clear and lift us, whatever the oppression that may have been caused." The realism, he added, might be taken as a necessary "correction to the flimsy, to which our literature has a tendency to recur."[22] In other words, Henley's work seemed to represent a deliberate reaction to

20 George Meredith, *Letters*, 2 vols. (New York, 1913), ii, 600.
21 "Heine on Crutches," *National Observer*, ix (1893), 344.
22 Meredith, *Letters*, ii, 412.

the literary despair of the 'seventies and the blue-china aestheticism of the 'eighties. And to a degree, Meredith's view was the right one. Yet every reaction implies an understanding of the principles to be rejected. If Henley took arms against a sea of troubles, he could not ignore its mainspring in the headlands of Victorian thought. He was no more able than Mill or Green, Mr. Stockton or Mark Rutherford, to root his philosophy in a firm religious faith. Intellectually and emotionally he found himself excluded from the mystic fervor of Carlyle, the vague but boisterous theism of Browning, the consistent Anglican orthodoxy of Charles Kingsley. For his activism, he was driven to seek new sanctions; and the nature of his personal experience combined with a new science to ensure that those sanctions would be biological.

PART I. DERIVATIONS

The sower must take his seedsheet and go afield into ground prepared for his ministrations; or there can be no harvest. The Poet springs from a compost of ideals and experiences and achievements, whose essences he absorbs and assimilates, and in whose absence he could not be the Poet.

—HENLEY

For the bookshop of William Henley in Gloucester, 1849 was an epic year. As on a seismograph, the fluctuations in local taste recorded themselves upon his ledgers. In February a fourth edition of *Modern Painters* sold well, despite its anonymity. And several weeks later it was joined by *The Seven Lamps of Architecture,* which disclosed the authorship of John Ruskin. By March Mrs. Trollope's sensational new novel, *The Lottery of Marriage,* had joined the bestseller lists. Then the *pièce de résistance* of the spring season—and probably indeed of the whole generation—the first number of *David Copperfield,* was announced for May Day. Safely launched, the Dickens serial rolled triumphantly down the months, growing in bulk and power and public estimation, until at its maturity it moved beyond time to the place of things perennial. Yet, whatever its taste for fiction, Gloucester was not deaf to the moral muse; Martin Tupper's *Proverbial Philosophy,* now almost a classic, had lost nothing of its appeal by July when a handsome reprint of the author's *Crock of Gold* arrived from London. Still, momentous or profitable as these works might prove to the bookseller, they were as nothing in comparison with the August arrival. For on the twenty-third of that month, Mrs. Henley was delivered of a first-born son. And William Ernest—as the child was christened—promptly became the bookshop's proudest acquisition. After his advent, the appearance in October of Currer Bell's *Shirley,* elsewhere so widely acclaimed, could not here but seem anticlimactic.

William Henley claimed no kinship with the Earls Henley of Northington nor with the fluent orator of Pope's second *Dunciad.* That he came of "ancient yeoman stock" was pedigree enough[1]; his sense of humor

---

[1] See Cornford, *Henley,* p. 22.

was too lively to attach much importance to the involutions of genealogy. Yet he could condone the vanity of his wife, Emma Morgan, who was inordinately proud of her descent from Joseph Warton, and who was sufficiently literate to appreciate the glory to which she by that descent was heir. Of her five sons, she saw fit to bless one with the poet-critic's name. If Anthony Warton, who made of himself a landscape painter, never achieved the eminence for which he was predestined, the salient fact yet remains that he had within him the creative impulse; and years later when "Bob" Stevenson met him in Paris, he was happily sharing in the struggles of artists more successful than himself[2]; his career was not a complete failure. The other children entered upon life without Anthony's singular advantage. One of them, surely the least gifted of the five, disappeared, nameless, into the turmoil of a busy age. Another, Nigel by name, conjoining a deep understanding of design and a patience with detail, rose to "the top of his chosen profession" as keeper of prints in the British Museum.[3] The youngest and most romantic of the boys was Edward John, born in 1861. Like Christian Buddenbrook, "Teddy" displayed from childhood an unholy faculty for mimicking his betters. Eventually he strutted his talents across a far-flung stage; he lived to see his name in bright letters on posters and marquees in London and New York, in Montreal and San Francisco.[4] Emma thus had five strong sons, each in his own way remarkable, yet each able to live in amity with his brothers. Surely her pride of lineage was not without foundation.

Throughout the 'fifties and 'sixties, William Henley pursued a precarious livelihood. The Victorians had lost nothing of their strenuous reading habits; they had gone

[2] For a photograph of A. W. Henley among his Parisian friends, see Will H. Low, *A Chronicle of Friendships* (New York, 1908), p. 208.

[3] See Elizabeth Robins Pennell, *The Life and Letters of Joseph Pennell*, 2 vols. (Boston, 1929), i, 269.

[4] See the report of an interviewer's conversation with E. J. Henley, *New York Dramatic Mirror*, xxxv (1896), 2.

so far as to relax their concept of Sabbatarianism in order to accommodate the Sunday perusal of lighter literature. But they were now finding new ways to circumvent book purchase. Mudie's Select Library had already begun to encroach upon the provincial bookseller's territory. Such competition intensified the difficulty of sustaining a growing family and left the elder Henley preoccupied with the problems of domestic finance. In the mid 'seventies he died penniless; and of his death, his poet-son had nothing to say. But the mother's passing in the late 'eighties was another matter. William Ernest arose from his watch by the deathbed to write the most impassioned of his elegies:

Dearest, live on
In such an immortality
As we thy sons,
Born of thy body and nursed
At those wild, faithful breasts,
Can give—of generous thoughts,
And honourable words, and deeds
That make men half in love with fate! . . .

Between the river and the stars,
O royal and radiant soul,
Thou dost return, thine influences return
Upon thy children as in life, and death
Turns stingless! What is Death
But Life in act? How should the Unteeming Grave
Be victor over thee,
Mother, a mother of men?

That such eloquence was something more than poetic intoxication, Edward John, three thousand miles from home, bore witness; by the news of his mother's death, the actor was "affected . . . almost to delirium."[5] In her artist-children, "half in love with fate," Emma Henley had engendered a lasting devotion; to the end she remained a symbol and an inspiration.[6]

[5] *New York Dramatic Mirror*, xxxv (1896), 2.

[6] See also the tribute of Robert Louis Stevenson, written in Honolulu, "*In Memoriam*, E. H.," *Scots Observer*, i (1889), 693.

Whatever may have been his father's shifting fortunes, William Ernest Henley read his boyhood quietly away in a Gloucester bookshop. Years later as self-appointed dictator of taste, he would revert again and again to the books that had been his first friends. It may be that his physical affliction, long before its true nature became apparent, had removed him from the society of boys his own age. In any case, the child turned at the outset from life to literature; and the romance that he imbibed from books, he brought to bear upon his actual experience. Once when he had attended a reading by Dickens in a crowded assembly hall, he had so fastened his eyes upon the lecturer's hand that he carried with him forever the image of a long white finger and a large flashing jewel.[7] Dickens the man became to him one with Dickens's own creations, one with Pickwick and Mrs. Gamp, one with Chuzzlewit and Sidney Carton; he remained "always an incarnation of generous and abounding gaiety, a type of beneficent earnestness, a great expression of intellectual vigour and emotional vivacity."[8] Woe it was to him who might prefer the viciously genteel Thackeray or that "Apotheosis of Pupil-Teachery" known as George Eliot.[9]

"I can," Henley wrote in his best-known essay, "certainly read my mother-tongue."[10] And, let who would dispute his taste, none could question his literacy. But from the beginning, he esteemed not less than native writers the great foreign romancers whom he first encountered in English translation. He valued beyond words "the friendship of the good Alonso Quijada" and the company of "old d'Artagnan."[11] If he missed the heroics of Homer, he found delight protean in the adventure of a thousand and one *Arabian Nights*. This, his Golden Book, he first knew in the rendition of Antoine Galland; a work of art, it seemed to him, beside

[7] See Cornford, p. 10.
[8] Henley, *Works*, IV, 8.
[9] *Works*, IV, 120.
[10] *Works*, II, 158.
[11] *Works*, IV, 84.

34

which the later versions of Payne and Burton were as mere ethnological curiosities. Its double columns of microscopic print strengthened rather than alienated his affection; they were an earnest of the more joy in store for him. The narrative of Zobeide, "alone in the accursed city whose monstrous silence is broken by the voice of the one man spared by the wrath of God as he repeats his solitary prayer," this ranked "with Crusoe's discovery of the footprint, in the thrilling moments of [his] life."[12] Galland's book was his passport to the enchanted kingdoms of "the magian East"; it was

> what is gallantest and best
> In all the full-shelved Libraries of Romance,—
> The Book of rocs,
> Sandalwood, ivory, turbans, ambergris,
> Cream-tarts, and lettered apes, and calendars,
> And ghouls, and genies—O, so huge
> They might have overed the tall Minster Tower
> Hands down, as schoolboys take a post!
> In truth, the Book of Camaralzaman,
> Schemselnihar and Sinbad, Scheherezade
> The peerless, Bedreddin, Badroulbadour,
> Cairo and Serendib and Candahar,
> And Caspian, and the dim terrific bulk—
> Ice-ribbed, fiend-visited, isled in spells and storms—
> Of Kaf! . . . That centre of miracles,
> The sole, unparalleled Arabian Nights!

This matter of Baghdad gave an extraordinary stimulus to his childish imagination. It brought wonderment and mystery to the sleepy grey city of his birth. It transformed Gloucester's prosaic cobbler, mending shoes at his shopdoor, into the wizened Leprechaun, cogitating the imponderables of scarlet destinies. One day the nine-year old strayed into the deserted showroom of a traveling Madame Tussaud's, where, "behind a fence of faded crimson cords," he chanced upon

12 *Works*, IV, 192-93.

A Woman with her litter of Babes—all slain,
All in their nightgowns all with Painted Eyes
Staring—still staring.

From these wax images he fled in terror; but down the dark streets their insufferable Painted Eyes followed him. For weeks they leered at him 'round the minster archways. They pursued him even unto Candahar; they branded him pariah in "the Palace of the King." Some thirty-five years later he could evoke the episode with a psychological validity comparable to the opening chapter of *Great Expectations*. Even as England's most vigorous "realist," he had retained much of his capacity for romance. Yet the time came when actualities far more terrible than Painted Eyes were to reshape his whole philosophy.

Never particularly robust of physique, Henley succumbed in his twelfth year to a disease which might have been diagnosed as tubercular arthritis, but about which the surgeons of Gloucester had no real understanding. His body had grown out of all proportion to his withered limbs. An insidious enemy gnawed mercilessly at his hands and feet. The normal Victorian remedy for this complaint was amputation; and the usual result of amputation was gangrene and consequent death. But the Victorian child was expected to meet such eventualities with courage. In *The Crofton Boys*, which appeared in 1856,[13] Harriet Martineau had depicted the ideal reaction to a surgical operation, one of the few in which the victim was spared gangrenous infection. It is unlikely that the young Henley heeded the deaf sybil, whose precepts his father almost certainly must have purveyed. Yet it is not unprofitable to examine her narrative as a commentary, not wholly conscious,[14]

[13] First separately published in 1856, but previously included in *The Playfellow*, 4 vols. (London, 1841), Vol. IV.

[14] Miss Martineau shows no desire to attack the prevalent surgical methods; she is concerned rather with the ideal "manly" reaction thereto.

on the barbarism of Victorian medical practice. Hugh Proctor, the hero of her fiction, has fractured his foot during a boarding-school squabble. His uncle comes with due solemnity to his bedside; and the model dialogue ensues:

"Oh, dear! oh, dear! Uncle, do you think it a bad accident?"

"Yes, my boy, a very bad accident."

"Do you think I shall die? I never thought of that," said Hugh.

"No; I do not think you will die."

"Will they think so at home? Was that the reason they were sent to?"

"No; I have no doubt your mother will come to nurse you, and to comfort you; but—"

"To comfort me? Why, Mr. Tooke said the pain would soon be over, he thought, and I should be asleep to-night."

"Yes; but though the pain may be over it may leave you lame. That will be a misfortune; and you will be glad of your mother to comfort you."

"Lame!" said the boy. Then, as he looked wistfully in his uncle's face, he saw the truth.

"Oh, uncle! they are going to cut off my leg."

"Not your leg, I hope, Hugh. You will not be quite so lame as that; but I am afraid you must lose your foot."

"Was that what Mr. Tooke meant by the surgeon's relieving me of my pain?"

"Yes, it was."

"Then it will be before night. Is it quite certain, uncle?"

"Mr. Annanby thinks so. Your foot is too much hurt ever to be cured. Do you think you can bear it, Hugh?"

"Why, yes, I suppose so. So many people have. It is less than some of the savages bear. What horrid things they do to their captives,—and even to some of their own boys! And they bear it."

"Yes; but you are not a savage."

"But one may be as brave, without being a savage. Think of the martyrs that were burnt! And they bore it!"

Mr. Shaw perceived that Hugh was either in much

less pain now, or that he forgot everything in a subject which always interested him extremely. He told his uncle what he had read of the tortures inflicted by savages, till his uncle, already a good deal agitated, was quite sick; but he let him go on, hoping that the boy might think lightly in comparison of what he himself had to undergo. This could not last long, however. The ringing pain soon came back; and as Hugh cried, he said he bore it so very badly, he did not know what his mother would say if she saw him. She had trusted him not to fail; but really he could not bear this much longer. . . .

"Don't let mother come," said Hugh.

"No, my boy, I will stay with you," said his uncle.

The surgeons took off his foot. As he sat in a chair, and his uncle stood behind him, and held his hands, and pressed his head against him, Hugh felt how his uncle's breast was heaving,—and was sure he was crying. In the very middle of it all, Hugh looked up in his uncle's face, and said,

"Never mind, uncle! I can bear it."

He did bear it finely. It was far more terrible than he had fancied; and he felt that he could not have gone on a minute longer. When it was over, he muttered something, and Mr. Tooke bent down to hear what it was. It was—

"I can't think how the Red Indians bear things so."

If for a time Henley escaped this ordeal, he was forever reminded of its imminence. The enemy gnawing at his bone would leave him no peace.

As far as a suffering child's attention could be diverted from his torment, Henley was engrossed in his studies at the Crypt Grammar School of Gloucester. This ancient institution, established by Burgess John Cooke in the year 1509 for the education of "certain poor boys,"[15] provided an inefficient counterpart to the Cathedral School, where the students, for the most part sons of prosperous tradesmen, hung blue tassels from their mortarboards, lest they be confused with their

[15] Henley, "T. E. B.," *Works*, II, 377.

indigent rivals. The Crypt had long since fallen upon evil days when the Chancery Commissioners in 1860 began inquiry into its abuses. The most effective among their reforms was the appointment of a new headmaster, Thomas Edward Brown.

"T. E. B." came to Gloucester trailing clouds of glory. He had graduated from Oxford with an enviable "double first" in Classics and Modern History.[16] He had held a fellowship at Oriel. He had been ordained deacon by Bishop Wilberforce. For five years he had served as Vice-Principal of King William's College in his native Isle of Man. At thirty he brought to the Crypt an unusual breadth of experience, a genuine enthusiasm, "a gift of exciting and a gift of teaching." But he also brought the temerity and the temper that were to be his own undoing. He was intolerant of opposition; and wherever he turned he found himself opposed. The Commissioners, like Mr. Gladstone a few years later, demanded that retrenchment accompany reform. The headmaster declared retrenchment quite impossible; he refused to accept inferior equipment; he declined to teach from outmoded, unreadable texts. Moreover, he was sufficiently ill-advised to battle with his overseers "in the local prints"; for he could, as Henley pointed out, "in nowise realise the kind of illiteracy—vain, fat-witted, beery, excessively conservative—into whose midst he had descended."[17] Inevitably, despite his talents, because of his talents, he failed. With evident relief he quitted the Crypt in September, 1863, to fill the post of Second Master at Clifton. There he remained in complete happiness for nearly thirty years, until "the Gloucester episode" had become a memory he did not choose to awaken.

From Henley's point of view, however, Brown's tenure of office had been an unqualified success,

[16] See *Works*, II, 378; also Selwyn G. Simpson, *Thomas Edward Brown* (London, 1906), p. 22.
[17] *Works*, II, 379.

since it made him known to me, and opened to me ways of thought and speech that—well! since it came upon me like a call from the world outside—the great, quick, living world—and discovered me the beginnings, the true materials, of myself. . . . What he did for me, practically, was to suggest such possibilities in life and character as I had never dreamed. He was singularly kind to me at a moment when I needed kindness even more than I needed encouragement.[18]

It was a memorable day when "T. E. B." announced examination grades, and again and again Henley's name led all the rest. It was the day of the first private colloquy between master and pupil, which marked the beginning of their mutual understanding; it was a day as meaningful in the boy's life as the first wonderful meeting with John Keble was significant in the life of Cardinal Newman. From his own library shelves Brown scooped down precious volumes available in no county bookshop. The youth went home laden with the best that men had thought and said, full of his master's courage and confidence. New horizons of literature stretched out before him; the mere act of living became to him something worthwhile, something worth even the price of endurance.

Henley's interest in books did not flag with the resignation of the man who had most stimulated him. In 1867, at the age of eighteen, he passed the local Oxford examination as a senior candidate with a far more than adequate knowledge of English letters. But his poverty and ill-health made the examination of little consequence. By the following spring he had grimly accepted the verdict of incompetent surgeons. In the small hospital at Smithfield they amputated his foot. Concerning these butchers and his reaction to them, he kept a stoic's silence. His only published reference to the operation occurs in a birthday letter of May, 1900, to his friend, Austin Dobson. His one consolation in the Smithfield

18 *Works*, II, 380.

tragedy, it appears, had been his discovery during con-
valescence of Anthony Trollope's *St. Paul's Magazine,*
in which were first printed Dobson's "Marquise" and
the "Story of Rosina."[19]

After the operation he went back to Gloucester where
he continued to live at home. Disillusioned with life, he
held faith in his books. Already he was reaching for
standards to guide his critical judgment. When Rossetti
in 1870 poured a Pre-Raphaelite vintage, "cooled a long
age in the deep delvèd earth," Henley turned instinctively to the sobriety of Pope.[20] But he was also beginning to express his own emotion in verse; and the earliest
of his poems linked him to the Victorian romantics
rather than the Augustan classicists:

> Life is bitter. All the faces of the years,
> Young and old, are gray with travail and with tears,
>   Must we only wake to toil, to tire, to weep?
> In the sun, among the leaves, upon the flowers,
> Slumber stills to dreamy death the heavy hours . . .
>   Let me sleep.

Obviously derivative in form and content, these lines
have nonetheless considerable biographical relevance.
They give some indication of Henley's state of mind
during the five years following the first operation. In
that time the disease had crept into his other foot; the
old pains had renewed their assault. His will to live
weighed lightly in the balance against his longing for
release. And yet there was left in him enough of the
spirit of Headmaster Brown to resist a petition for complete surrender. When the surgeons told him early in
1873 that he must submit to a second amputation, he
scorned their harsh decree. Wearily, grimly, he began
the trek to Edinburgh.

[19] See Alban Dobson, *Austin Dobson, Some Notes* (London, 1928),
p. 166.
[20] See Cornford, p. 7.

✒ CHAPTER 3. IN HOSPITAL. EDINBURGH: 1873-1875

SIR JAMES SIMPSON may have wondered in the last year of his life whether his long labors had been in vain. He could not doubt his accomplishment; the "perchloride of formyle" that he had introduced to a generation skeptical as to its religious propriety had now become the standard prelude to every surgical operation. He remembered his triumphs: how the first grateful mother to use the drug in childbirth had named her resultant daughter Anaesthesia, how the Queen herself had placed the royal approval upon his discovery during her confinement with Prince Arthur, how the late Consort had talked to him enthusiastically "of *Punch*, Scotland, and chloroform."[1] His battle lay behind him; he had made a distinct and valid contribution to the arts of healing. Yet his victory was incomplete as long as surgeons refused to see the relation of dirt to disease. A painless incision could not avert a painful infection. If the number of operations for minor ailments had multiplied tenfold, pyaemia and gangrene had increased proportionately.

In 1869 Sir James issued a sweeping indictment of Victorian medical practice. His ten-year survey of London, Glasgow, and Edinburgh hospitals revealed that two out of every five simple amputations and two out of every three amputations through the thigh proved fatal.[2] And there were no statistics to tell "of the unspeakable agony patients suffered as the gangrene gnawed at the living flesh, of the sharp cries of pain and the tragic prayers breathed to the Divine mercy for the speedy gift of death."[3] Yet the statistics themselves were

1 See Eve Blantyre Simpson, *Sir James Y. Simpson* (Edinburgh, 1896), pp. 60, 63, 139.
2 See G. T. Wrench, *Lord Lister* (New York, n.d.), pp. 130, 163. In figures: of 2,089 simple amputations, 855 resulted in death; in Edinburgh, of 371 amputations, 161 resulted in death.
3 Wrench, p. 130.

sufficiently alarming to the investigator. "Do not these terrible figures," he asked, "plead eloquently and clamantly for a revision and reform of our existing hospital system?"[4] Unfortunately, however, his mind was no longer open to new ideas; he was unprepared to accept the only reform worth the name. He might have seen in Joseph Lister, who arrived in Edinburgh shortly after the publication of the report, an immediate solution to the problems he had raised. Instead he saw only a commendable enthusiasm misguided by an irrational faith in carbolic acid.

Early in 1865 Lister encountered a French periodical article concerning putrefaction, wherein the author, Louis Pasteur, contended that sepsis usually arose not from within the wound itself but from the action on the wound of minute organisms omnipresent in the atmosphere. According to this "germ theory," sepsis might be ended by the destruction of microbes already feeding on the tissue and the exclusion of others from the tissue. Lister accepted the theory as valid and at once began his search for a suitable antiseptic chemical. When he heard of the salutory effects of carbolic in removing the sewage odor at Carlisle, he obtained a quantity of the acid for experiment in his Glasgow ward. So crude of form was the dark, tarry liquid that it seemed insoluble in water. Yet, applied to the wound, it produced effects little short of miraculous; it irritated the tissue, induced bleeding, and then formed a crust with the blood. This was the first "antiseptic scab," a hermetic seal against contamination from the air. Lister's enthusiasm led him at first to exaggerate the virtues of carbolic. With more refined phenol he evolved successively a carbolic spray, a carbolic gauze, a carbolized putty.[5] He cleansed his instruments in watery carbolic acid and demanded that all assisting surgeons wash their hands in the same fluid.

[4] Quoted by Wrench, p. 132.
[5] See Sir Hector Clare Cameron, *Reminiscences of Lister* (Glasgow, 1927), pp. 16, 23; also Sir William Watson Cheyne, *Lister and His Achievement* (London, 1925), p. 37.

His methods of disinfection should not, of course, be reduced to a single formula. But the notion of a universal panacea struck the popular imagination; and we find a would-be Scottish Byron rhyming in *ottava rima*:

> To work out this solution, tooth and nail,
>> With skill and labour at it Lister went,
> Fully determined that he should not fail;
>> And many an hour, and day, and week he spent,
> Racking his very brains till he grew pale,
>> And making many an experiment,
> Until at last he found—it made him placid—
> The true *solution* in Carbolic Acid.[6]

Whatever the misinterpretation of his work,[7] Lister himself had a broad faith in the power and purpose of the antiseptic treatment. From that faith he drew courage to operate on a close relative, affected with carcinoma of the breast, at a time when other surgeons would have shrunk from the operation through fear of almost certain septic poisoning. Through that faith he was ultimately to revolutionize the concept of "hospitalism."

Lister cast his inaugural address at the Royal Edinburgh Infirmary in the form of a challenge. Pitting the Old Medicine against the New, he told both young internes and seasoned practitioners that, thanks to the researches of Pasteur, "surgery becomes something totally different from what it used to be."[8] Professor Hughes Bennett, the "master of the microscope," sat impatiently through the lecture and then rose to refute the whole absurd germ theory. His colleagues agreed that the new head surgeon was being most impractical. Thus, from the beginning, Lister found the weight of authority against him. But opposition gave impetus rather than rebuff to his unbending will. Like the husband in Trollope's novel, though with better reason, he

6 Quoted by Wrench, p. 272.
7 Lister claimed to use much less carbolic acid than those who imitated him; he insisted not on one antisceptic, but rather on a belief in the germ theory. See Cameron, p. 33.
8 Quoted by Wrench, p. 208.

knew he was right; his smile was "sweet with certain-
ties." Within four years he had transformed a backward
infirmary into the foremost of British hospitals. The
wind from the Pentland Hills, blowing freshly through
the long corridors, commingling with the pungent odor
of carbolic, testified as to the extent of his achievement.
Yet he could scarcely have done so much alone. While
Simpson and Bennett scoffed at his campaign, the students upon whom depended the future of his cause
rallied beneath the banner of reform. "I have always,"
he said years later, "I have always had youth on my
side."[9] From August, 1873, he had also on his side, for
what it was worth, the confidence of the young Henley.

Lister found his theories of antiseptic surgery nowhere more valid than in the treatment of the large
abscesses that originate in the tuberculous caries of the
joints. Henley's case was, therefore, one to which he
brought a lively interest and a tried experience. In it
lay his opportunity of proving the new methods to a
patient already mangled by the old. He would, he was
sure, be able to scrape the infection from the bone without the danger of concomitant gangrene; there would
be no second amputation. But the patient must not expect immediate recovery; such treatment was inevitably
a long and painful process, at times testing human endurance to its limits.

Henley passed twenty months under Lister's care in
the Edinburgh Infirmary; and towards the end of that
time he recorded, as dispassionately as possible, his re-
actions, physical and psychological, to his environment.[10] His verses, *In Hospital*, polished and repolished
over a period of thirteen years, present a microcosm of
his whole biography. They reveal, ceaselessly at work,
a dialectic of denial and assent; and they point towards
the final synthesis, which, generally speaking, was to

[9] Quoted by Cameron, p. 38. *Cf.* Wrench, p. 205.
[10] Henley dates the hospital period, "August, 1873–April, 1875,"
"Hospital Sketches," *Voluntaries for an East London Hospital*, collected by H. B. Donkin (London, 1887), p. 148.

determine his whole subsequent attitude to reality. In the sense of the title-page caption,[11] they belong among the most personal poems in the language.

But, apart from any subjective connotation, the greatness of the Hospital sequence lies in the detachment from which it derives an independent dramatic unity.[12] For the appeal is calculated to be aesthetic; the author is in no way solicitous of the reader's sympathy. With amazing dispassion he follows the protagonist of his tragicomedy from his arrival in the morning mists at the bleak hospital until his departure for the high noon of life in the open air. He re-visions through the eyes of the character he has created the "gruesome world" of "Scissors and lint and apothecary's jars," and he feels once more his initial revulsion:

> The gaunt brown walls
> Look infinite in their decent meanness.
> There is nothing of home in the noisy kettle,
> The fulsome fire.
>
> The atmosphere
> Suggests the trail of a ghostly druggist.
> Dressings and lint on the long, lean table—
> Whom are they for?
>
> The patients yawn,
> Or lie as in training for shroud and coffin.
> A nurse in the corridor scolds and wrangles.
> It's grim and strange.[13]

As if from a "third-personal" vantage point, he beholds the youth waiting,

[11] Henley heads *In Hospital* with a quotation from Balzac, "*On ne saurait dire à quel point un homme, seul dans son lit et malade, devient personnel.*"—*Works*, I, 2.

[12] *In Hospital* has the dramatic "curve" of complication and denouement. The action is confined to distinct scenes or settings, the first of which is entitled "Enter Patient."

[13] As it appears in the *Works*, *In Hospital* has been fully revised. This poem is roughly equivalent to Sonnet III, "The Ward," *Cornhill Magazine*, xxxii (1875), 121.

waiting for the knife.
A little while, and at a leap I storm
The thick, sweet mystery of chloroform.

Follows the operation itself, described without a trace
of hysteria or self-pity:

> You are carried in a basket,
>   Like a carcase from the shambles,
>   To the theatre, a cockpit
> Where they stretch you on a table.
>
> Then they bid you close your eyelids,
>   And they mask you with a napkin,
>   And the anaesthetic reaches
> Hot and subtle through your being.
>
> And you gasp and reel and shudder
>   In a rushing, swaying rapture,
>   While the voices at your elbow
> Fade—receding—fainter—farther. . . .

The aftertaste of anaesthetic, "foully sweet," lingers on
as he recovers consciousness; and a "dull, new pain . . .
grinds [his] leg and foot." All this is but a prelude to the
lonely vigil, the dark weeks of uncertainty, when

> Lived on one's back,
> In the long hours of repose,
> Life is a practical nightmare—
> Hideous asleep or awake.
>
> Shoulders and loins
> Ache — — !
> Ache, and the mattress,
> Run into boulders and hummocks,
> Glows like a kiln. . . .
>
> All the old time
> Surges malignant before me;
> Old voices, old kisses, old songs
> Blossom derisive about me;
> While the new days

47

> Pass me in endless procession:
> A pageant of shadows
> Silently, leeringly wending
> On . . . and still on . . . still on!

Recovery comes slowly, and with it, the ability to transcend the suffering, to find mental release in the Balzacs brought by friends,

> Big, yellow books, quite impudently French.

Better still, there is romance in the hospital itself. The sailor tells of blockade-running in the American war, of mud and chains, and Negroes on the wharf at Charleston, "Poor old Dixie's bottom dollar." The ploughman in his "crackling, hackling" voice sings

> of bonnie lasses
> Keeping sheep among the heather.

Even in the Lady-probationer, her of the "dark eyes and shy, . . ignorant of sin," there must be hidden wells of life:

> Her plain print gown, prim cap, and bright steel chain
> Look out of place on her, and I remain
> Absorbed in her, as in a pleasant mystery.
> Quick, skilful, quiet, soft in speech and touch . . .
> "Do you like nursing?" "Yes, Sir, very much."
> Somehow, I rather think she has a history.

And there is high inspiration in the heroism of Lister himself, "the Chief" who

> seems in all his patients to compel
> Such love and faith as failure cannot quell.
> We hold him for another Herakles,
> Battling with custom, prejudice, disease,
> As once the son of Zeus with Death and Hell.

But the distant piping of the barrel organ engenders an irresistible nostalgia for "the blessèd airs of London"; and April, reaching through the "grimy, little window," brings a passing tingle to the blood and an abiding sense

of frustration. Into his ultimate escape, the invalid pours
a lifetime of thwarted joy:

> Carry me out
> Into the wind and the sunshine,
> Into the beautiful world.
>
> O, the wonder, the spell of the streets!
> The stature and strength of the horses,
> The rustle and echo of footfalls,
> The flat roar and rattle of wheels!
> A swift tram floats huge on us. . .
> It's a dream?
> The smell of the mud in my nostrils
> Blows brave—like a breath of the sea!
>
> As of old,
> Ambulant, undulant drapery,
> Vaguely and strangely provocative,
> Flutters and beckons. O, yonder—
> Is it?—the gleam of a stocking!
> Sudden, a spire
> Wedged in the mist! O, the houses,
> The long lines of lofty, gray houses,
> Cross-hatched with shadow and light!
> These are the streets. . .
> Each is an avenue leading
> Whither I will!
>
> Free. . . !
> Dizzy, hysterical, faint,
> I sit, and the carriage rolls on with me
> Into the wonderful world.

So in childlike ecstasy, the patient is recalled to a life
beyond the gray hospital corridors.

Considered as an artistic unit, the sequence represents an achievement in objective writing; for the author,
even though drawing upon his own experience, is constantly above his subject; he remains always in complete
control of his materials. But, in a broader sense, there
can be no objective art; the dispassionate technique is

49

itself a reflection of the artist's point of departure.
is is pre-eminently true of the verses *In Hospital,*
where the poet's vision throughout is conditioned by his
fierce will to live. With the renascent feeling that the
victory is worth the struggle, Henley looks at his world
with a new intensity. If he is to understand existence at
all, he must reduce it to its lowest common denominator.
Accordingly, for the nebulous imagery of his earliest
verse, he substitutes a concretion of detail, a sharpness
of outline. As if continually obsessed with the dread that
life may be slipping from him, he clings with an over-
zeal to the basic physical sensations. On his release, it
is the sudden superabundance of acute impression—
"the flat roar and rattle of wheels," "the smell of the
mud," "the gleam of a stocking"—that swells his being
with a joy unutterable. He focuses a hard, white light
on the surfaces of things, till he has laid bare their very
essences. At its best, his work satisfies the standards of
steel engraving; each shadow is deliberately placed;
each line takes telling effect. Within the Infirmary,
there is little or no distracting color[14]; all is black and
white and indeterminate gray. The flame is blanketed
in smoke; the night lamp is half-guarded. A single splash
of brightness is garish against the drab background;
from his bedclothes, "Case Number One" stretches a
sick foot,

> Swaddled in wet, white lint
> Brilliantly hideous with red.

Only the visitor is brown-eyed, "rich-tinted," "radiant
with vivacity"; but then he is something of an "Appari-
tion," come by some romantic whim from a far fairy-
land. The real Edinburgh beyond the hospital windows
is colorless as the gray ward; beneath an April sun, the
poet sees only etched design in the "lofty, gray houses,
Cross-hatched with shadow and light."

[14] There are very few color words: "gray" occurs nine times in the
twenty-nine poems; "brown," twice; "green," twice, but as a noun,
meaning "grass" in the world *outside*; "red," twice, of blood.

50

In the same intense visualization lies the power of the unique verse-portraits, by virtue of which Mr. Alfred Noyes has ranked Henley as a major poet.[15] The exigencies of the sonnet-form demand unusual economy of expression; only the significant detail remains to suggest the total character. But Henley moves easily within the medium. He forces himself to reduce a complex individuality to its elements. He contrives to find a guiding principle behind each of the persons he depicts. Lister lives by "his unyielding will," his dedication to an heroic ideal. The staff-nurse, old-style Mrs. Porter,[16] exercises at all times the benevolent despotism to which thirty years' experience entitles her. Miss Mitchelson, her new-style counterpart, is conscious of an innate superiority; even her "plainest cap is somehow touched with caste." The house-surgeon is neither more nor less than a genial Philistine. Nevertheless, despite a fundamental simplicity of conception, all of these emerge as complete, life-size human beings. Among the most vivid portraits in the hospital gallery is that of Miss Abercromby, the sister of charity. More than the others, perhaps, it indicates the amused detachment from which the poet makes his appraisals:

Her little face is like a walnut shell
With wrinkling lines; her soft, white hair adorns
Her withered brows in quaint, straight curls, like horns;
And all about her clings an old, sweet smell.
Prim is her gown and quakerlike her shawl.
Well might her bonnets have been born on her.
Can you conceive a Fairy Godmother
The subject of a strong religious call?
In snow or shine, from bed to bed she runs,
All twinkling smiles and texts and pious tales,
Her mittened hands, that ever give or pray,

[15] See Noyes, "The Poetry of W. E. Henley," *Contemporary Review*, cxxi (1922), 205.

[16] Identified in an unpublished letter, attached to a copy of *In Hospital* in the University of Toronto Library, written by Dr. G. A. Gibson, who was in charge of Henley's ward, and dated from Edinburgh, 1913.

Bearing a sheaf of tracts, a bag of buns:
A wee old maid that sweeps the Bridegroom's way,
Strong in a cheerful trust that never fails.

In the matter of technique the comparison is once again
with the graphic arts. This is a genre study done entirely
without color, a simple design in black and white. But
the portrait implies infinitely more than a sense of arrangement. Its strength rests on an objective sympathy,
a "negative capability," an aesthetic aloofness guided
by an understanding of fundamental character values.

Henley's concern with the hospital drama was not
less disinterested than Miss Abercromby's charity. His
psychological recovery demanded a sacrifice of the desire for personal escape to the claims of an interdepend-
ent society. He turned from his own miseries to the
problems of his fellow inmates. He lent a willing ear to
the reminiscences of Kate the Scrubber; and he marveled at the courage that had sustained her through
trial and tribulation. He learned case histories more
sordid than his own. And he succeeded in diverting the
whole gaunt ward with anecdote and song and the
favorite tunes he played upon a tin whistle. He could
never forget the hospital New Year when he had piped
"The Wind That Shakes the Barley," while Kate, a little
the worse for liquor, had tripped a sprightly measure,
herself the whole ballet. Again and again he rallied two
small boys, Roden Shields and Willie Morrison, with
games of war and "droll ditties" sung "to a rollicking air
and in a strong Irish accent":

Ah, hurrah, brave boys! we're all fur marching;
Some fur Spain and some fur Belgim.
Drums are bating, colirs are flying,
Which among us thinks of dying?
Love, farewell! darlint, farewell!
We're all fur marching. Love, farewell!

His mere range of moods fascinated the children, who
peered at him from the next cot, critical, admiring, half-
afraid. Years later when Roden had become a Glasgow

52

tailor, he remembered Henley's mirth and his gloom, his singing and the long hours of silence when

> I used to watch him looking hard at the roof, thinking, smiling, and frowning as if he saw nice things and talked to people. I never dared question him in these moods, but I resolved when I was a man I would get pillows at my back and a desk fitted to my bed, and read and smile and frown like Henley.

Roden and Willie often wondered why he passed so much of his time in writing; and they were not quite satisfied by his reply that he had many letters to send to his grandmother.[17] Yet they could scarcely have known the labor involved in the verses which were recording his experience.

The decision to accept Henley's "Hospital Outlines" for publication in the *Cornhill* was one of the "boldest ventures" in the editorial career of Leslie Stephen. Such crude realism would certainly offend feminine delicacy; and "Thou shalt not shock a young lady" was, he said, "the first commandment that he had to enforce."[18] Though the acceptance itself must have meant a good deal to the convalescent poet, Stephen carried his kindness still further. While on a lecture tour to Edinburgh, he sought out Henley at the Infirmary. In a letter home he told Mrs. Stephen of "an interesting visit to [his] poor contributor" and of a plan to help him. "I went," he explained, "to see Stevenson this morning, Colvin's friend, . . and am going to take him there this afternoon. He will be able to lend him books, and perhaps to read his Mss. and be otherwise useful. So I hope that my coming to Edinburgh will have done good to one living creature."[19] His hope was not misplaced, for that afternoon Colvin's friend came with him to the hospital.

---

[17] See Roden Shields, "A Blurred Memory of Childhood," *Cornhill Magazine*, NS xix (1905), 227, 228.

[18] Quoted by Frederic William Maitland, *The Life and Letters of Leslie Stephen* (London, 1906), p. 266.

[19] Quoted by Maitland, p. 250. The letter is undated.

Both of them were moved by the sight of "the poor fellow" who "sat up in his bed with his hair and beard all tangled, and talked as cheerfully as if he had been in a King's palace or in the great King's palace of the blue air."[20] Saturday, the thirteenth of February, 1875[21] —it was in many respects the most significant single day in Henley's life.

Stevenson came to the Infirmary not once but many times. A remarkable figure, he seemed to Henley, something of an anachronism, a Victorian Villon, "Buffoon and poet, lover and sensualist." Passionate, impudent, energetic, he was able to make himself "useful" in ways that Stephen could not have imagined. He encouraged the patient's effort to learn Spanish and Italian; and he brought to the hospital Mrs. Fleeming Jenkin who consented to give free lessons in German. Each week he came laden with paper-bound French novels at which Miss Mitchelson looked askance. Not all his usefulness, however, was of so academic a character; for his interest in Henley went beyond their mutual love of foreign literature. He was concerned with the individual; "Henley," he said, "has an immortal soul of his own."[22] Consequently, he sought out kindred spirits in whose presence Henley might realize his own true self. The friends whom he introduced into the ward, Charles Baxter, James Walter Ferrier, Sir Walter Grindley Simpson— these men opened vistas of life outside the invalid's narrowed experience. But above all others, "Lewis"[23] him-

[20] *Works of Robert Louis Stevenson,* 27 vols. (New York, 1911), XXIII, 98.

[21] For this dating, see Rosaline Masson, *The Life of Robert Louis Stevenson* (Edinburgh, 1923), p. 250.

[22] Stevenson, *Works,* XXVII, 317.

[23] "Lewis": R. L. S. was baptized Robert Lewis Balfour Stevenson. Henley refused to recognize the name "Louis," which he considered sheer affectation; he, therefore, always wrote of "Lewis." In reality, the change in spelling had a quite different origin. Thomas Stevenson, it appears, ordered the new spelling when the local Radical, Lewis— odious to the Conservative Thomas—was elected town councillor. See Eve Blantyre Simpson, *Robert Louis Stevenson's Edinburgh Days* (London, 1898), pp. 16-17.

self engendered an eagerness to accept the world for
what it was, to seek from the drab reality the latent
romance of living.

In April, just two months after Leslie Stephen's first
visit, Henley was removed from the Infirmary to Porto-
bello on the Firth of Forth. There Louis called every
afternoon with the family carriage to drive him through
the green countryside. Henley would ride in silence, his
eyes fixed on "the cherry-blossoms bitten out upon the
black firs, and the black firs bitten out of the blue sky."
"The look of his face," said Louis, "was a wine to me."[24]
On the Bridges they always lingered a moment to let
Henley "enjoy the great *cry* of green that goes up to
Heaven out of the river beds"; and sometimes he would
ask, " 'What noise is that?'—'The water.'—'O!' almost in-
credulously; and then quite a long time after: 'Do you
know the noise of the water astonished me very much?' "
Louis was "much struck by his putting the question
twice."[25] But Henley would continue to put such questions until the end; he would never outgrow his childlike wonder. His release from the hospital had meant
only that he would inflict his assertion, his positive faith,
on a generation of half-believers. His voice would cut
stridently across a late Victorian defeatism:

> Free. . . !
> Dizzy, hysterical, faint,
> I sit, and the carriage rolls on with me
> Into the wonderful world.

[24] Stevenson, *Works*, xxiii, 107.
[25] xxvii, 316-17.

CHAPTER 4. *"INVICTUS."* THE GRAMMAR OF ASSENT

STEVENSON knew nothing of the Henley who had lain, in the first Edinburgh months, helpless upon a hospital cot, doubtful as to the value of life itself. He could remember only a maimed Prometheus, scorning the decrees of angry gods. His description of the penny whistle and its effect on the ward attains an almost Henleyan grandiloquence:

> Small the pipe; but O! do thou,
> Peak-faced and suffering piper, blow therein
> The dirge of heroes dead; and to these sick,
> These dying, sound the triumph over death.
> Behold! each greatly breathes; each tastes a joy
> Unknown before, in dying; for each knows
> A hero dies with him—though unfulfilled,
> Yet conquering truly—and not dies in vain.
>
> So is pain cheered, death comforted; the house
> Of sorrow smiles to listen. Once again—
> O thou, Orpheus and Heracles, the bard
> And the deliverer, touch the stops again![1]

This poem is highly pertinent to any account of the Henley-Stevenson relationship. It depicts the piper as Louis wished to see him and as he himself desired to appear. And thereby it suggests the attitude towards pain of two youths who had each suffered greatly and whose common friendship was grounded in a personal experience, and a mutual defiance, of physical handicap. Critically, their tastes, their prejudices, their philosophies of living can only be measured against an incessant battle with tubercular disease. For neither was long free from some sort of bodily torment. Their war was never won; but while a shred of life remained, neither would admit it lost. In the South Seas, a month

---

[1] Stevenson, *Works*, XVI, 122-23.

before the end, Stevenson, looking back upon his struggle, wrote to George Meredith:

> For fourteen years I have not had a day's real health; I have wakened sick and gone to bed weary; and I have done my work unflinchingly. . . . I was made for a contest, and the Powers have so willed that my battle-field should be this dingy, inglorious one of the bed and the physic bottle. At least I have not failed, but I would have preferred a place of trumpetings, and the open air over my head.[2]

Had he also been at heart "the Anxious Egotist,"[3] Henley might have written a like statement. Certainly his attitude to the contest and the ruling Powers, as expressed in his verse, was identical. And he could appreciate the sincerity behind Stevenson's histrionics. No sooner had he, freed from the hospital, recovered his own health, than he was called upon to serve as nurse to Louis, "in secret, hard by the old Bristo port."[4]

The tubercular germ that blighted both their lives may conceivably have had some effect on their powers of imagination. The thesis that "the toxins of the disease act in some way as a stimulus to the brain" might seriously be defended.[5] A recent writer on the subject, Dr. L. J. Moorman, believes that the victim of tuberculosis feels himself isolated, "no longer wholly subject to the world's conventional authority, and consequently . . . is in a position to exercise a free critical spirit." And another investigator contends that the patient, craving "a full and active life, . . lives in an atmosphere of feverish eagerness to seize the fleeting moments before they pass."[6] Such theorists would explain only too easily the creative restlessness of Stevenson or the daring icono-

2 *Works*, xxiv, 362-63.
3 See Henley, "R. L. S.," *Pall Mall Magazine*, xxv (1901), 510.
4 *PMM*, xxv, 506.
5 See *Journal American Medical Association*, xcix (1932), 2297.
6 See Lewis J. Moorman, *Tuberculosis and Genius* (Chicago, 1940), "Introduction," pp. xii, xiii.

clasm of Henley. They would cast new light upon the
carpe diem motif of lines as cavalier as

> O, gather me the rose, the rose,
>   While yet in flower we find it,
> For summer smiles, but summer goes,
>   And winter waits behind it!

> For with the dream foregone, foregone,
>   The deed forborne for ever,
> The worm, regret, will canker on,
>   And Time will turn him never.

And undoubtedly these elucidations would carry weight
in particular cases. But when Dr. Moorman suggests a
general correlation between the decline of power in contemporary literature and the decrease in the prevalency
of tuberculosis,[7] we begin to suspect the validity of even
his special pleadings. A "Magic Mountain," we might
argue, would tend to preclude rather than guarantee a
literary renaissance. If disease gave Henley and Stevenson a heightened perceptivity, it as demonstrably weak-
ened their efforts at self-expression. The best work of
the English poet is forever to a degree overdeliberate;
his richest music is marred by false tonalities. Likewise,
the most graceful prose of the Scots storyteller is somehow strained in its mere precision.

As commentator on the invalid's modes of thought,
the psychologist is both more convincing and more provocative than the physician. Where Dr. Moorman seeks
evaluation, Dr. Adler contents himself with analysis. He
assumes as obvious the interdependence of body and
mind and proceeds at once to infer the self-involvement
of physical debility and mental health. The invalid, constantly aware of his inferiority, becomes neurotic, subject to an endless emotional conflict; despising his own
weakness, he covets a strength beyond his attainment.
He, therefore, tends to measure all things by their weak

[7] In support of this theory, Moorman quotes a colleague, Dr.
Jacobson, p. xv.

and strong propensities. As he always "apperceives
after the analogy of a contrast" and usually "only recognizes and gives value to relations of contrast," he dichot-
omizes the whole world "according to the Scheme 'Tri-
umph-Defeat,'" and ultimately according to "the only
real 'antithesis' of 'man-woman.'" His values thus con-
veniently simplified, he raises a defensive "masculine
protest" against uncertainty, insecurity, indecision, in
short, against every token of "effeminacy."[8]

The concept of the "masculine protest" would appear
to have considerable relevance to the cases of Henley
and Stevenson. While Dr. Adler's theory of causation is
somewhat problematical, the effects that he outlines are
patent in the style and thought of both writers. Antithesis is integral to the very structure of Stevenson's essays.[9]
And Henley's verse is obsessed with dichotomies, while
his prose revels in the odious comparison. In both,
though with significant divergences, the dominant attitude is that of vigorous masculinity. Stevenson's stories
inculcate the principles of strenuous living. And Henley's imperial propaganda carries virilism to almost
pathological extremes.

The dedication to *Virginibus Puerisque* makes mani-
fest the author's outlook on reality; addressing "My Dear
William Ernest Henley," Stevenson writes:

> Times change, opinions vary to their opposite, and still
> this world appears a brave gymnasium, full of sea-
> bathing, and horse exercise, and bracing, manly virtues;
> and what can be more encouraging than to find the
> friend who was welcome at one age, still welcome at
> another? Our affections and beliefs are wiser than we;
> the best that is in us is better than we can understand;
> for it is grounded beyond experience and guides us,
> blindfold but safe, from one age to another.

[8] See Alfred Adler, *The Neurotic Constitution* (New York, 1917),
pp. 24-25, 86, 99-101.

[9] See Alice D. Snyder's stimulating article, "Paradox and Antithesis
in Stevenson's Essays," *Journal of English and Germanic Philology*,
xix (1920), 540-59.

The world is thus a good place, "a brave gymnasium," where the manly individual can trust his basic instincts as stronger and wiser than his faculties of intellection. Such a philosophy leads inevitably to a repudiation of convention; a morality of taboos has ceased to be moral; the "masculine protest" demands a positive ethic for active living. In "A Christmas Sermon" Stevenson places gentleness and cheerfulness, "the perfect duties," before all morality. For it was "the moral man, the Pharisee, whom Christ could not away with," the uncharitable censor of other men's well-intentioned mistakes. The true Christian accepts cheerfully the inescapable fact that human beings are from the outset doomed to mortality; and without illusion he wages, undaunted to the end, a losing battle. Then, if he has struggled manfully, he will content himself with the epitaph: *"Here lies one who meant well, tried a little, failed much."* Death will have no bitterness to the happy warrior of whom it can be said: "There, out of the glorious sun-coloured earth, out of the day and the dust and the ecstasy—there goes another Faithful Failure!"

To Stevenson, then, the challenge of life lies not in the possible victory but rather in the inevitable defeat. Satisfaction of desire means the death of the spirit. Growth, struggle, assertion—these are their own rewards. Pain is but a goad to the restless soul, driving it away from the bypaths of indolence, prodding it ever on towards complete, but unattainable, realization. Happiness ceases to be the object in living. Life becomes the end in itself; other end is unimaginable in a world whose law is change and death, a world where all souls must learn the "high doctrinality of suffering."[10] The bad man is the slothful, only too willing to stagnate in the weeds of comfortable respectability. The good man is, by implication, the gallant warrior who enters the lists with steady hand and indomitable will. The bad man is

[10] See Stevenson's letter to Henley, dated Dec. 11, 1879, *Works*, xxvii, 128-29.

the pessimist who questions the purpose of the battle. The good man is the optimist who accepts the struggle, who delights in it as did the forebears of the good Fleeming Jenkin—"They had all the gift of enjoying life's texture as it comes; they were all born optimists."[11] Renunciation is the cardinal sin; the ascetic is the chiefest of transgressors. Where Arnold found the Grande Chartreuse a refuge for the "last of the people who believe," Stevenson sees in monastic orders a contemptible escape from reality. Our Lady of the Snows serves only to inspire a longing for the active life:

> O to be up and doing, O
> Unfearing and unshamed to go
> In all the uproar and the press
> About my human business! . . .
>
> For still the Lord is Lord of might;
> In deeds, in deeds, he takes delight; . . .
> Those he approves that ply the trade,
> That rock the child, that wed the maid,
> That with weak virtues, weaker hands,
> Sow gladness on the peopled lands,
> And still with laughter, song and shout
> Spin the great wheel of earth about.[12]

In comparison with Arnold's "Stanzas," these didactic couplets are little more than doggerel. But they are nonetheless representative of Stevenson's ethical philosophy. They provide a crude illustration of the "masculine protest" that colors most of his work and thought.[13]

Henley did not write Christmas sermons. He admired Stevenson the stylist; but he had no sympathy with the

---

[11] Works, xviii, 37.

[12] "Our Lady of the Snows," Works, xvi, 132-33.

[13] Apparently Stevenson, like the Keats of the revised Hyperion, thought the life of action preferable to the life of art. Will H. Low thought it "most distressing that Stevenson should continually have . . . viewed his undeniable endowment as an artist to be inferior to the other avocations of man."—See "An Epilogue to an Epilogue," Modern Essays, Christopher Morley, ed. (New York, 1925), p. 416.

"artist in morals," the "Shorter Catechist of Vailima."[14]
He came to see the intellectual impotence of mere "vo-
calisings about duty." And yet, in spite of himself, he
subscribed emotionally to Stevenson's credo. If he wrote
in less explicit terms concerning the principles of strenuous living, he not the less frequently embodied those
principles in his own creative and critical works.

Anticipated by the triumphant finale to the verses *In
Hospital*, Henley's "Echoes of Life and Death" furnish
forth the most complete lyrical statement of his self-
assertive philosophy. Whereas the Hospital poems are
relatively impersonal units in a dramatic sequence, the
"Echoes" make no pretense at objectivity. In them the
poet sings endless variations on his central theme, the
incomparable romance of living:

> At whatever source we drink it,
>   Art or love or faith or wine,
> In whatever terms we think it,
>   It is common and divine. . . .

The Past was goodly once, and yet, when all is said,
The best of it we know is that it's done and dead. . . .
Duty and work and joy—these things it cannot give;
And the Present is life, and life is good to live. . . .

> The nightingale has a lyre of gold,
>   The lark's is a clarion call,
> And the blackbird plays but a boxwood flute,
>   But I love him best of all.

> For his song is all of the joy of life,
>   And we in the mad, spring weather,
> We two have listened till he sang
>   Our hearts and lips together.

Life is good and the poet clings to it with grim tenacity.
But his very ardor reminds him that the goodness is
passing:

[14] Henley, *PMM*, xxv, 508.

> Fill a glass with golden wine,
>   And while your lips are wet
> Set their perfume unto mine,
>   And forget,
> Every kiss we take and give
> Leaves us less of life to live.

Yet man cannot afford to doubt; to question life is to squander its brief divinity:

> We must live while live we can;
>   We should love while love we may.
> Dread in women, doubt in man . . .
>   So the Infinite runs away.

These are the echoes of life calling unto man to fulfill himself in the brave gymnasium of time. But to every call from life, there comes the answering echo of death. For death is the one reality from which there is no escape. It is the grim denouement to the comedy of tears:

> Madam Life's a piece in bloom
>   Death goes dogging everywhere:
> She's the tenant of the room,
>   He's the ruffian on the stair.

> You shall see her as a friend,
>   You shall bilk him once or twice;
> But he'll trap you in the end,
>   And he'll stick you for her price.

> With his kneebones at your chest,
>   And his knuckles in your throat,
> You would reason—plead—protest!
>   Clutching at her petticoat.

The echoes of death are not always so suggestive of Holbein's macabre *Totenbilder*. But they are always acceptant. There is in them no rebellion against the inevitable. And occasionally the resignation rises to the level of transcendent mysticism, where life and death coalesce into a larger design:

63

I am the Reaper.
All things with heedful hook
Silent I gather.
Pale roses touched with the spring,
Tall corn in summer,
Fruits rich with autumn, and frail winter blossoms—
Reaping, still reaping—
All things with heedful hook
Timely I gather.

I am the Sower.
All the unbodied life
Runs through my seed-sheet.
Atom with atom wed,
Each quickening the other,
Fall through my hands, ever changing, still changeless,
Ceaselessly sowing,
Life, incorruptible life,
Flows from my seed-sheet.

Maker and breaker,
I am the ebb and the flood,
Here and Hereafter.
Sped through the tangle and coil
Of infinite nature,
Viewless and soundless I fashion all being.
Taker and giver,
I am the womb and the grave,
The Now and the Ever.

Thus the ultimate antithesis resolves itself. Life and death cease to be the eternal antinomies. The one becomes unintelligible without the other; both play essential parts in the pattern of existence.

As poetry, "I Am the Reaper" attains the calm acceptance characteristic of Henley's last and mellowest verses. But it is scarcely representative of the poet's outlook on life in the spring of 1875. It conveys nothing of the fierce assertiveness that carried a jubilant youth out from an Edinburgh hospital into the wonderful world. In the expression of a "masculine protest" against pas-

sivity, it hardly compares with the strident *"Invictus,"*
which dates from the same year:

> Out of the night that covers me,
>   Black as the Pit from pole to pole,
> I thank whatever gods may be
>   For my unconquerable soul.
>
> In the fell clutch of circumstance
>   I have not winced nor cried aloud.
> Under the bludgeonings of chance
>   My head is bloody, but unbowed.
>
> Beyond this place of wrath and tears
>   Looms but the Horror of the shade,
> And yet the menace of the years
>   Finds, and shall find, me unafraid.
>
> It matters not how strait the gate,
>   How charged with punishments the scroll,
> I am the master of my fate;
>   I am the captain of my soul.

In its context as epilogue to the hospital drama, *"Invictus"* thus acquires a significance far beyond its value
as an isolated unit. It marks the invalid's triumph over
physical handicap. It grounds an activist philosophy on
a personal Darwinism, a necessary faith in the survival
of the biologically fit.

In a lecture of 1893 entitled "Ethics and Evolution,"
Thomas Henry Huxley warned his auditors that cultural collapse must surely attend a continued belief in
"the gladiatorial theory of existence." If society was to
endure, he said, man must learn to distinguish between
records of zoological research and guide books to moral
conduct. Of educated people he demanded spiritual
wakefulness; and in support of his demand, he cited
the high resolve, the indomitable will of Tennyson's
Ulysses. By the 'nineties Henley and Stevenson had also
begun to suspect the inadequacy of a purely physical
basis for the activist ethic. The worship of life implied

ultimately the deification of the universal Life. Accordingly, Stevenson wrote prayers at Vailima; and Henley recanted the violence of *"Invictus"*:

> Think on the shame of dreams for deeds,
> The scandal of unnatural strife,
> The slur upon immortal needs,
>   The treason done to life:
>
> Arise! no more a living lie,
> And with me quicken to control
> Some memory that will magnify
>   The universal Soul.

If this later theism encouraged reflection, it also placed upon the individual a new responsibility for active living, a regret for the dreams that might have been deeds. Stevenson's lay morals did not lessen his love of vigor; they gave him rather a new insight into character. In his last and greatest novel, he drew the heroic Gilbert Elliott, defiant, to the death, of the robber band threatening his life and property. And by the last lines of that novel, the last lines that Stevenson ever wrote, he conjured up a scene of tempestuous passion, "unprovoked, a wilful convulsion of brute nature. . . ." Similarly, that Henley had modified *"Invictus"* did not mean that he had repudiated his assent. Agnostic or theist, he remained as eager for the full life as he had been in the first month of his release from hospital; he could still chant:

> Life—life—let there be life!
> Better a thousand times the roaring hours
> When wave and wind,
> From the Arch-Murderer in flight
> From the Avenger at his heel,
> Storm through the desert fastnesses
> And wild waste places of the world.

As literary critic, as political editor, he appeared to the end the unshriven Giaour, impatient of the languorous repose. But his inner emotional development was less consistent, less assured, than his outwardly fierce demeanor might have suggested. The "masculine protest" indicated a realization of the ambivalence of values, of weakness commingling with strength. And the long, self-conscious search for style betrayed his feeling of uncertainty and his consequent desire for unequivocal expression. The will to live was strong, often because the fear of death was stronger.

PART II. THE SEARCH FOR STYLE

Lutte avec le carrare,
Avec le paros dur
    Et rare,
Gardiens du contour pur. . . .

Sculpte, lime, cisèle;
Que ton rêve flottant
    Se scelle
Dans le bloc résistant!

—GAUTIER

THE appearance of the "Hospital Sketches" in the *Cornhill* had encouraged Henley to think of himself as the poet. Now released from the Infirmary, he concluded that a Circumstance, less "fell" than he had feared, was intending him to see with the poet's eye and to speak in the poet's voice. From his garret high above Princes Street he heard the sea wind whistling like organ music through the chimney pots of Edinburgh. In the evening he saw the terraced rows of the Old Town spread out below him in the dark, bejeweled with lamps, and far to the west the menacing Castle silhouetted against a silver sky. He looked poetically out over the same sordid city that long before had amazed and delighted and disgusted a querulous Matthew Bramble. And poetically he made of his observation lyric and sonnet.

Louis read his verses with approval; and in July, 1875, he sent a selection from them to Sidney Colvin, suggesting that the "lovely" melodies were "not altogether without some trace of [his] influence."[1] Yet for all his romantic charm, Louis was forever the Scot; and as such, he attained a practicality almost beyond Henley's comprehension. If he praised the poetry, he taught the poet that in prose lay his livelihood. By precept and example, he proved that journalism itself might be treated as an art. Accordingly, Henley turned his gaze from the hills beyond to the publishing houses below. Though he kept by him always his "pipes pandean" and through them gave utterance to his deepest emotion, he sought his career elsewhere. Only after he had won repute as editor and critic could he gain audience for his descriptions of "the implacable night" and the "sinister seduction of the Moon."

It was probably through Stevenson's efforts that Hen-

1 Stevenson, *Works*, xxvii, 113.

ley obtained his first commission as a professional man of letters. Late in the year 1875, he agreed to contribute several articles on French literature to the Ninth Edition of the *Encyclopaedia Britannica*. Of these the short account of André Chénier was alone sufficiently considerable to warrant the printing of the author's initials. Yet the "Chénier" itself, as the earliest of Henley's critical estimates, already indicates the first principles of his literary judgment. Chénier, he wrote,

> was five-and-twenty, and at heart a Greek. The Idyllists and Anthologists were his masters. From their styles did he compound his own; and from them did he learn the exquisite purity of form, the admirable restraint, the chastened vigour of thought and diction, that render him pre-eminent among modern poets.

In a sense, to be sure, this represents nothing more than the conventional view of the classic French lyrist. Yet it bears closely upon a study of Henley's apprenticeship. It suggests the ideals—restraint of expression and purity of form—towards which he as a prose stylist would struggle. For "style" had now become his major concern. His hospital reading had borne fruit; and he found himself at six-and-twenty an authority on the incomparable Frenchmen. He knew and admired the French critics; he sprinkled his copious talk with French interjection; he strove to round the epigram, to make the period French in manner and movement. With Louis he analyzed page upon page of Stevensonian exposition and discussed at length the necessity of *le mot juste*. For over two years he met regularly with Fleeming Jenkin to debate in heated argument the exactitude of language and the nuance of idiom.[2] Anxious that his world should be coherent, he saw in the conscious simplicity of Gallic prose "the last refuge of complexity."

In Edinburgh Henley found few periodicals responsive to his and Stevenson's artistic journalism. Before

[2] See John A. Steuart, *Robert Louis Stevenson*, 2 vols. (Boston, 1924), I, 233.

long he was sending reviews to London; and some of these, duly cut by "clever editors," were appearing anonymously in literary supplements. He grew more and more impatient with the whole Scottish scene. Once Louis had taken him into the West Highlands, where he had wondered at the white cottages and the heather and the "noise of running water." But Louis himself was more at home in France than Scotland; and he spent long weeks with Will Low among the artists of Barbizon. Perhaps envious of his friend's travel, certainly dissatisfied with his own progress as reviewer, Henley longed to follow his manuscripts southward. For some months he had been reconciled to the north by the dark-eyed Anna, daughter of Edward Boyle and Marianne Mackie, to whom he wrote sweet songs of love and Maytime. Eventually, however, it was his devotion to Anna that drove him back to England, whence alone he might expect sufficient income to support an intended bride. His departure was but an earnest of his resolve:

In the year that's come and gone, dear, we wove a tether
All of gracious words and thoughts, binding two together,
In the year that's coming on with its wealth of roses
We shall weave it stronger yet, ere the circle closes.

To Stevenson, London meant Colvin and Edmund Gosse and the Savile Club—good friends, good conversation, good wine. To Henley, in the fall of 1877, it meant none of these things. If it held for him his whole future, it tried him first with poverty and disappointment. His father, the bookseller of Gloucester, had died penniless; and upon him, as the eldest of the children, devolved the care of the family. For such of his articles as were not rejected, he was glad to accept whatever pittance he was offered. In later life he could recall the depths of his want, his weariness, his hunger; to Leslie Cornford and to Mrs. Pennell he told how once he and his brother Anthony, wandering half-famished through

73

Leicester Square, had come upon the shilling which alone had procured for them that day's bread.[3] If he escaped the grosser indigence of Gissing, he yet had some experience of the miseries of Grub Street.

In the hour of need, the good Samaritan appeared. This was Robert Glasgow Brown, who had worked with Stevenson on the *Edinburgh University Magazine* and who now sought to promote a literary weekly in England.[4] Shortly before the Christmas of 1877, he appointed Henley to the editorship of *London* and so afforded the young reviewer the first considerable opportunity in a distinguished journalistic career. Reassured financially and heartened spiritually by Brown's expression of confidence, Henley straightway telegraphed to Anna the news of his good fortune and proposed marriage. Thereupon he returned to Edinburgh; and Miss Boyle became Mrs. Henley.

The haste with which the editor entered upon married life betrayed the intensity of his feeling rather than the impulsiveness of his nature. In the twenty-five years of mutual sympathy that followed, Henley had little cause to deem his decision ill-considered; time served only to increase his devotion. Until the end Anna shared in his every triumph and defeat; she nursed him through sickness; she suffered, and even understood, his short temper; she encouraged and inspired his writing, with the "beautiful serenity" of Agnes Wickfield and a sense of humor and realism quite her own. Unlike the more aggressive, temperamental Fanny Stevenson, she countered her husband's active prejudice with passive tolerance; she interfered neither with his work nor his friends; she softened his vigorous "masculine protest," indirectly, but effectively, through the mere example of feminine reserve. Unobtrusively she deepened and widened Hen-

[3] See Cornford, pp. 30-31; and for a slightly altered version of the story, *cf.* Elizabeth Robins Pennell, "William Ernest Henley, Lover of the Art of Book-making," *Colophon* (1931), Part V, Section 9, p. 4.

[4] See Masson, *Stevenson*, p. 164.

ley's whole philosophy. Justly proud of his choice, the poet courted her romantically until the last; she remained to him always his beloved *"Châtelaine."*[5]

Under Henley's direction *London* survived little more than a year. Oscar Wilde saw the cause of its decease in the editor's genius for editing a periodical out of existence.[6] Alice Meynell, on the other hand, could explain its untimely death only by assuming that the gods must too dearly have loved it.[7] Hers was both the kinder and the wiser judgment; for, in its time, *London* was indeed a remarkable magazine. It anticipated the *National Observer* both in its attacks on Gladstone and in the brilliance of its literary contributions. Besides occasional pieces by Grant Allen and James Runciman and Andrew Lang, there appeared in it, unsigned, a number of Henley's poems and many of the brief essays later to be included in his *Views and Reviews*. Moreover, it carried in three successive issues three parts of Stevenson's *Virginibus Puerisque*; and from June 8 to October 26, 1878, it printed all of the *New Arabian Nights*. But whether because of its editorial technique, or the gods' delight in it, or the poor reception of Louis's fantasies,[8] its days were numbered. By the spring of 1879, Henley was once again a "free-lance" journalist.

Success or failure, *London* established Henley's reputation as a "gentleman of the press." His vigorous and mannered personality had intruded itself upon the conventional drabness of Fleet Street. During the 1878 visit of the *Comédie française*, he was to be seen day after day, perched in the reviewer's stall at the Gaiety

[5] This was Henley's sobriquet for Anna; see E. V. Lucas, *The Colvins and Their Friends* (London, 1928), p. 139.

[6] For Wilde's opinion of Henley's various periodicals, see Wilfred Hugh Chesson, "A Reminiscence of 1898," *Bookman*, xxxiv (1911), 393.

[7] See Alice Meynell, "Mr. W. E. Henley's Poems," *Merry England*, xi (1888), 95.

[8] See Cornford, *Henley*, p. 32, and *cf.* Cornford, *Robert Louis Stevenson* (Edinburgh, 1899), p. 51.

Theatre; "I thought of him," wrote William Archer, then just beginning his own career, "as a maimed Berserker dropped [there] by some anachronistic freak of destiny."[9] And his talents were not less striking than his appearance. He was invited to submit literary and dramatic criticisms to the *Pall Mall Gazette* and the *St. James's Gazette,* to the *Saturday Review* and the *Athenaeum.* He met and admired Frederick Greenwood; he knew and despised John Morley. But whatever his prejudices, he could no longer afford independence. If he wished to sell his manuscripts, he had now to align his own capricious judgment with the standards of unaesthetic journalists. Time and again his enthusiasms were thwarted. He complained to Colvin of his wasted effort:

> The *Pall Mall* Meredith well nigh killed me; and last night I'd to see *Nicholas Nickleby* and do a notice ere I went to bed. I wrote a very decent little article, but I won't ask you to read it. I don't know how much will be left of it. A brutal and licentious editor, and so on. . . .![10]

At times he questioned whether or not he had in him at all the stuff of the critic. Once when Greenwood had given him "a rasping lecture on Style," he wrote in despair and disgust:

> I am afraid, my dear Mr. Sidney Colvin, that I am found out at last. Privately, I've always known I wasn't a critic; but I fancied I had concealed the fact with some success. Then Meredith spotted me; what *he* wanted was "criticism"; and now here's the good greenwood reechoing the same pathetic overword. . . . Please tell me in your next what criticism is; where it is to be procured; how they sell it; and whether . . . there's any reduction on taking a quantity.[11]

Morley's silent rebukes were considerably harsher than

[9] See C. Archer, *William Archer* (New Haven, 1931), p. 80, n.
[10] Quoted by Lucas, *The Colvins,* p. 114.
[11] Page 115.

Greenwood's verbal strictures. Henley had been greatly excited by Swinburne's *Songs of the Springtides*—"the book's an ecstasy of exaggeration, a rapture of superlatives. Such a son of Thunder and small beer I never did see." But Morley remained cold alike to the ecstatic *Songs* and to the Henleyan hyperbole; and Morley as editor was at liberty to discard the whole review. "I am positive," Henley told Colvin,

> he has suppressed my Swinburne altogether and my Blackmore as well. I am very sorry indeed, for if it is so, it means ruin. . . . I shall go and see Morley tomorrow, and ask about the French plays. If they, too, are to be done on approval—*bon soir!* . . . In the meantime, *j'ai des amis et j'ai une femme*—and life is—well, it's devilish enviable.[12]

Rejections so arbitrary brought undeniable disappointment; but they did not mean complete "ruin." Every failure was more than compensated by a new success. Norman Maccoll, editor of the *Athenaeum*, declared the seven-column article on Dickens a little masterpiece. And George Meredith eagerly sought out the critic who, in fetching him "a lusty clout o' the head," had savagely told "the blasted public" with how great a genius they had to reckon.[13]

Sidney Colvin felt that Henley could ascribe his reverses as reviewer only to his own deplorable style. A long letter of friendly advice listed innumerable defects in diction and eccentricities of structure:

> "Fillip up" is slang and bad form. . . . "Elocutionist" is a beastly Yankeeism. "A something of" is not English at all. . . . "Intelligence of," for "comprehension of" or "insight into," is bizarre, and more Italian than English. To be bizarre, that is in one word your temptation; whether it is the knack or the habit which you have to unlearn. To afford to be bizarre, as I have often told you,

12 Pages 122, 124-25.
13 See Meredith, *Letters*, i, 299, and R. E. Sencourt, *Life of George Meredith* (London, 1929), p. 233.

77

you must be Charles Lamb with his genius and his leisure for polishing. . . .[14]

However Henley received such criticism, he must have resented the insinuation that any of his articles had been "filliped up" in slovenly haste. For he was a self-conscious craftsman; and his sins were painstakingly committed. His writing resembled that of Pater's Flavian, who used words with the same purpose and to the same effect; he was intent upon "weighing the precise power of every phrase and word, as though it were precious metal, disentangling the later associations and going back to the original and native sense of each,—restoring to full significance all its wealth of latent figurative expression, reviving or replacing its outworn or tarnished images. . . . For words, after all, words manipulated with all his delicate force were to be the apparatus of a war for himself." In his use of archaism, of root meaning, of contemporary slang, he was fully deliberate; and at the end of his period of apprenticeship, he could sincerely beg William Sharp to believe that "my efforts—of simplicity, directness, bluntness, brutality even—are carefully calculated, and that 'crude' —which means raw—if it means anything at all—is a word that I'd rather not have applied to me."[15] If his *bizarrerie* did not wholly satisfy his own standards, he was yet unprepared to accept the merely conventional prose commended to him as its antidote. In his quest for models he went further afield than the approved and respectable reviews. He advised Colvin to read what Louis Veuillot had to say in *Les Odeurs de Paris* concerning Gautier and the sin of pleonasm.[16] For he felt that the Slade Professor himself might profit from a few lessons in "original" composition. Like Stevenson and

[14] Quoted by Lucas, p. 121.

[15] Quoted by Elizabeth A. Sharp, *William Sharp* (London, 1920), p. 140.

[16] See Lucas, *The Colvins*, p. 114; and *cf.* Louis Veuillot, *Les Odeurs de Paris* (Paris, 1867), p. 245.

78

Flavian and Flavian's creator, he stemmed from a generation almost morbidly aware of its own attributes, a generation to whom manner and matter were inseparable categories.

Henley's concern with form in the early reviews implied no inability to grapple with substance. Rightly or wrongly, he considered himself a critical force. And when Colvin's *Landor* appeared in 1881, he tempered his praise with sharp censure. Colvin was entirely mistaken in his view of Landor as a great dramatic artist; and it seemed best to tell him so:

> The truth is, my Colvin, that your admiration for Landor as a writist has somewhat got the better of your better judgement as a critic of the creative in art. . . . I wish we had talked these "Conversations" over more fully, book in hand, ere you wrote. And I wish, too, that I'd minded my *Count Julian* better. The scene you quote ought to have settled the dramatist with you forever. . . . No man could gravely write and as gravely publish that for passion and for a scene, and ever become a dramatic poet. . . .
>
> It's for this reason that I love my Epicurus and his two girls and my *Caesar and Lucullus*. There's no pretence at drammy there. It's all Landor pure and simple; everything is apt, cheerful, stately, discursive, broken, impetuous, irrational, and splendid; a talk of golden-mouthed gods. Decidedly, I am a better judge of literature than you. Than you, even! O Sidney Colvin, M.A., and Fellow of Trinity! Than you—than you—than you! Think of that, and be confounded.
>
> Now I'll go drink a whiskey and soda, and go to bed. I am tired, and it's doosid late. Good night.[17]

Henley thus knew what he believed, and spoke it with the self-assured finality of a parting "Good night." Bernard Shaw was therefore scarcely just when he described him as "an Elizabethan, . . a man with an extraordinary and imposing power of saying things, and with

[17] Quoted by Lucas, pp. 137-38.

79

nothing whatever to say."[18] Yet there was a grain of truth in the Shavian indictment. Though assuredly a sound and penetrating critic of other men's art, Henley tended in his creative work of this middle period to regard form as its own *raison d'être*. His experiments with style in prose, in verse, and in drama were designed to give him mastery of the verbal medium, that he might better articulate the ideas and ideals of his maturity.

[18] Quoted by Archibald Henderson, *George Bernard Shaw* (London, 1911), p. 213.

✍§ CHAPTER 6. "WHITE MARBLES, WHITER WORDS." VERSE, FORMAL AND FREE: 1875-1888

JOHN HENRY NEWMAN's refusal to look upon the tricolor of a French vessel lying at anchor in Algiers was oddly of a piece with Thomas Carlyle's praise of the heroic Goethe. Despite Newman's later apology, despite Carlyle's sympathetic study of the Revolution, the Victorians as a people persisted in averting their gaze from France and in turning their affections towards Germany. Arnold, it will be remembered, though among the earliest to champion French culture, invented the legend of the Goddess Lubricity; and his moral condemnation of the Republic was born of inbred Victorian prejudice. The overcoming of this bias on three fronts, the intellectual, the aesthetic, and the political, was coterminous with a decline of high Victorianism, a token that the great age was outgrowing itself. Intellectually, the French positivists were already half-acceptable to the timorously agnostic 'sixties. Aesthetically, as we have seen, French prose-style made its impress on the late 'seventies, though it was not until the "decadent" 'nineties that the subject-matter of French realism excited any considerable imitation. Politically, the prejudice was never vanquished—never at least during the Queen's lifetime. A month before Henley's 1901 article on Stevenson, the *Pall Mall Magazine* divulged the French plans for an invasion of England. The momentous alliance with France was a distinctly Edwardian achievement.

While the English Pre-Raphaelites ignored their French contemporaries, they shared certain ideals with the Parnassian group. Both schools were concerned with factual detail; both distrusted purely subjective verse; both wished to effect a liaison between poetry and the plastic arts. But these resemblances were more or less accidental; and the points of divergence were basic. Ostensibly "designed as a protest against some ruling tendencies in the Art of the time," *The Germ* proved far less revolutionary than the Brotherhood imagined. To Henley "the best thing" in it was the work of the Pre-Raphaelite sister, "the wonderful woman—so far and away the greatest poetess our England has ever had"[1]; and Christina Rossetti's lyrics, fresh as they were in emotion, departed not at all from the recognized structural traditions of romantic love poetry. Neither in *The Germ* nor in his later volumes did Rossetti himself register any distinct protest against the formal looseness of Victorian verse. No one "fully alive to the perfection, and at every point awake to the completeness of *Kubla Khan*" could read "Sister Helen," for example, "without wishing that at least a third of it had remained unwritten—or at least unprinted." Rossetti and his confreres had "failed in two several arts," simply because "the means of expression—the grammar of style and words and paint—were only to be achieved through greater difficulty and distress than [they] cared to face."[2] That this is much too harsh a judgment, "the fundamental brainwork" of *The House of Life* furnishes ample proof. Yet Henley's general position is tenable; Rossetti was not consistently concerned with the discipline of form. *Firmilian* had scotched the snake, not killed it; the prolixity of Spasmodic verse persisted into the 'seventies. *Fifine at the Fair* outrhymed the most intrepid reader's endurance; and *The Earthly Paradise* mirrored worlds without end.

Unlike the Pre-Raphaelites, the French Parnassians revolted self-consciously against the facile composition of their romantic predecessors. They were, by will and by endowment, "minor poets" in the fullest sense of that label; they despised the profuse strains of Lamartine, not merely because they themselves were incapable of such abundance, but also because they sincerely be-

[1] Henley, "The Pre-Raphaelite Brethren," *PMM*, xxv, 259.
[2] Henley, *Works*, iv, 344-45.

lieved "unpremeditated art" a contradiction in terms. As conceived by Gautier who formulated the Parnassian ideal, verse was to be as deliberate and incisive as sculpture, and its contours were to be as sharply defined. A dictum so dogmatic could exert little direct or immediate influence upon Victorian English poets. But it provided a distinct stimulus to a whole group of French artisans whose wares in due course found their way across the Channel. Théodore de Banville made the demand for severe craftsmanship most explicit in his *Petit Traité de Poésie française*, which clearly explained the stylistic values of the old French forms; and he proceeded to illustrate his analysis by the exemplary *Trente-six Ballades joyeuses pour passer le temps, composées à la manière de François Villon.* Reaching London in the mid 'seventies—at a time, by the way, when in Paris Verlaine's Symbolist verse was already displacing the work of the Parnassians—these two books aroused sudden and singular enthusiasm. In them a number of the younger Victorians saw a necessary corrective to Spasmodic fluidity. Edmund Gosse felt impelled to write in the *Cornhill* for July, 1877, "A Plea for Certain Exotic Forms of Verse," wherein he argued that the Spasmodic School had left "a baneful influence, a tradition of formlessness behind it." But, he added, "the invertebrate rhapsodies of Sydney Dobell, so amazing in their beauty of detail and total absence of style, are now impossible. We may lack his inspiration and insight, but we understand far better than he the workmanship of the art of verse." Some years later Gosse traced the origins of the old French vogue to a general desire "for the support of a more rigid and disciplined metre," which led many a young man to experiment in the light of Banville's rigid rules.[3] Highly sensitive to trends in taste, Henley shared in this omnipresent desire for form. Like Osric,

[3] See a letter from Gosse, dated 1911, quoted by Helen Louise Cohen, *Lyric Forms from France* (New York, 1922), p. 82.

he, too, in his *Bric-à-brac*, whistled "the tune of the time."[4]

Henley's earliest exercises in formal verse appeared anonymously in *London*. Andrew Lang, one of the signing contributors to that ill-fated periodical, disclosed the secret of the authorship to Austin Dobson who warmly expressed his delight in the ballades and rondeaus. In a letter acknowledging the compliment, Henley apologized profusely for having dared attempt a *Ballade à double refrain* before Dobson: "Unfortunately, however, in an evil hour I listened to Clement Marot, and rushed upon my fate. . . . I can only console myself for my indiscretion by looking upon your Ballade as the dawn, and mine as the darkest hour which is supposed to precede it."[5] So solemnly might one Etonian have discussed with another the problem of precedence at the wicket. For to Henley the French forms were a game conducted according to accepted rules; and Dobson was the accredited master. He was the gentleman-amateur who carried his skill easily, without affectation. "In writing of this sort," said Henley, "there is a certain artistic good-breeding whose like is not common in these days. We have lost the secret of it: we are too eager to make the most of our little souls in art and too ignorant to do the best by them; too egoistic and 'individual,' too clever and skilful and well informed to be content with the completeness of simplicity."[6]

Though thus impressed by Dobson's firm sense of control and his true literary *savoir-faire*, Henley was yet under no illusion as to the essential artifice of the formal convention. He could scarcely ask high passion of Banville's *Ballades*, where the refrains danced an artful, innocent minuet:

[4] Quoted by Henley himself on the title page of *Bric-à-brac*.
[5] From a letter of Feb. 28, 1878, quoted by Alban Dobson, *Austin Dobson*, pp. 103-4.
[6] *Works*, IV, 111.

Ici tout est couleur de la rose . . .
Il sied de boire en l'honneur des pucelles . . .
Embarquons-nous pour la belle Cythère . . .
Vive Margot avec sa jupe rouge . . .
Diane court dans la noire forêt . . .
Moi, j'en ris, les jours de soleil . . .
O lèvre rouge, ô belle fleur de sang . . .
Je ne veux du tout que ma mie . . .
Pourquoi je vis? Pour l'amour du laurier . . .
Je suis un poète lyrique . . .

His estimate of such work mingled appreciation and amusement. Banville, he said, "writes of 'Pierrot, *l'homme subtil*,' and Columbine, and '*le beau* Léandre,' and all the marionettes of that pleasant puppet-show which he mistakes for the world, with the rhetorical elegance and distinction, the verbal force and glow, the rhythmic beauty and propriety, of a rare poet; he models a group of flowers in wax as passionately and cunningly, . . as if he were carving the Venus of Milo, or scoring Beethoven's 'Fifth.' "[7] In "artistic good-breeding," "rhetorical elegance," "verbal force," Henley found his ideals as a writer of verse and prose; the discipline of rigid form would, he knew, leave him thoroughly "grammared" in style.

Among the late Victorian architects in rhyme, Henley occupied a distinguished place. In one respect at least, it was a unique place; for Henley alone sympathized with the discipline of technique while explicitly satirizing its results. He employed the extremely complex villanelle form, merely to demonstrate to the reader that he is to expect little or nothing of the villanelle's contents:

> A dainty thing's the Villanelle;
> Sly, musical, a jewel in rhyme,
> It serves its purpose passing well.

[7] *Works*, IV, 108.

A double-clappered silver bell
  That must be made to clink in chime,
A dainty thing's the Villanelle;

And if you wish to flute a spell,
  Or ask a meeting 'neath the lime,
It serves its purpose passing well. . . .[8]

Thus the artisan freed himself from the obligation of
seeking out sound subject-matter. Inspired by Dobson,
he might weave rhymes about "A Flirted Fan" and "A
Fan from Rimmel's," or, better still, he might turn rondeau after rondeau upon that most savory of subjects,
"My Meerschaum Pipe." His concern was all with

> Fountains that frisk and sprinkle
> The moss they overspill;
> Pools that the breezes crinkle;
> The wheel beside the mill,
> With its wet weedy frill;
> Wind-shadows in the wheat;
> A water-cart in the street;
> The fringe of foam that girds
> An islet's ferneries;
> A green sky's minor thirds—
> To live, I think of these. . . .
>
> Dark aisles, new packs of cards,
> Mermaidens' tails, cool swards,
> Dawn dews and starlit seas,
> White marbles, whiter words—
> To live, I think of these!

"White marbles, whiter words," these afforded relief
from the intensity of vision that Henley brought to the
"Hospital Sketches"; they provided a temporary escape

[8] Reading these verses as an attempt at serious poetry, Gerard Man-
ley Hopkins attacked Henley and the formalists in general; see Claude
C. Abbott, ed., *Letters . . . to Robert Bridges* (London, 1935), II,
276-77. *Cf.* Stevenson's letter to Henley from Lake Saranac, 1887:
"Damn your villanelles and everybody's" (*Works*, XXVII, 235). *Cf.*
also Henley's triolet on the triolet, Gleeson White, ed., *Ballades and
Rondeaus* (London, 1887), p. 221.

from the hammer rhythm of pain and pleasure, of hope and fear that pulsed through the "Echoes of Life and Death." "Let us be drunk," he cried,

> Let us be drunk, and for a while forget,
> Forget, and, ceasing even from regret,
> Live without reason and despite of rhyme,
> As in a dream preposterous and sublime,
> Where place and hour and means for once are met.
>
> What is the use of effort? Love and debt
> And disappointment have us in a net.
> Let us break out and taste the morning prime . . .
>   Let us be drunk. . . .

And there was an intoxication in the white words themselves, in the refrains singing *à la* Banville, in orderly array, like well-behaved fairies:

> With Sir Love among the roses . . .
> I loved you once in old Japan . . .
> Fate's a fiddler, Life's a dance . . .
> If it could be always May! . .
> 'Tis the symphony of Spring . . .
> Midsummer nights! O midsummer nights! . .
> O Vanity of Vanities . . .

These were dream voices, "preposterous and sublime," from the Never-Never Land of no regrets. The very titles of the *Bric-à-brac* poems suggested the distance of their themes from reality: "Ballade of a Toyokuni Colour-print," "Ballade Made in the Hot Weather," "Ballade of Truisms," "Of Antique Dances," "Of Spring Music," "Of Ladies' Names." If such verses had little to say, they yet said it with matchless grace. No one attempting the difficult art of verse translation ever surpassed Henley's rendition of Ronsard's *"Ainsi qu' aux fleurs la vieillesse,"* which recaptured all the cultivated naïveté of the original:

> And lightly, like the flowers,
>   Your beauties Age will dim,
> Who makes the song a hymn
>   And turns the sweets to sours!

87

Alas! the chubby Hours
  Grow lank and grey and grim,
And lightly, like the flowers,
  Your beauties Age will dim.

Still rosy are the bowers,
  The walks yet green and trim.
  Among them let your whim
Pass sweetly, like the showers,
And lightly, like the flowers.[9]

Where the borrowed inspiration of Ronsard was lacking, the smoothness and dexterity remained even in patterns most likely to defy directness of expression. "Henley's 'Double Ballade on the Nothingness of Things,' seventy-two lines long," writes Mr. Louis Untermeyer, "is one of the most astonishing of these endurance contests."[10] To judge by the poem's theme, the "double-ballade" form was selected merely as an exercise in virtuosity; as such, it served its purpose passing well.

While perfection of form and vapidity of substance are the rule in Henley's book of *Bric-à-brac*, there are yet one or two noteworthy exceptions. A portrait-sonnet about an old fishwife, which follows a sketch of "an enchanting little Israelite, . . with hair escaped from some Arabian night," strikes a note of realism reminiscent of the *In Hospital* verses. Likewise, the burlesque rondeau, "Villon's Straight Tip to all Cross Coves," a masterly recreation of the fifteenth century French underworld in terms of traditional English cant, breaks the mood of sentimental romance:

Suppose you screeve? or go cheap-jack?
  Or fake the broads? or fig a nag?
Or thimble-rig? or knap a yack?
  Or pitch a snide? or smash a rag?

9 White, ed., *Ballades and Rondeaus*, p. 139.
10 Louis Untermeyer and Carter Davis, *Poetry, Its Appreciation and Enjoyment* (New York, 1934), p. 403.

Suppose you duff? or nose and lag?
Or get the straight, and land your pot?
How do you melt the multy swag?
Booze and the blowens cop the lot. . . .

But two poems reach a coalescence of manner and matter above all others. One of these is the "Ballade of Dead Actors," later dedicated to "Teddy" Henley:

Where are the passions they essayed,
And where the tears they made to flow?
Where the wild humours they portrayed
For laughing worlds to see and know?
Othello's wrath and Juliet's woe?
Sir Peter's whims and Timon's gall?
And Millamant and Romeo?
Into the night go one and all. . . .

The curtain falls, the play is played:
The Beggar packs beside the Beau;
The Monarch troops, and troops the Maid;
The Thunder huddles with the Snow.
Where are the revellers high and low?
The clashing swords? The lover's call?
The dancers gleaming row on row?
Into the night go one and all.

Here in the concrete visual imagery of the refrain, the world of make-believe impinges for once on the world of reality; the stage of artifice becomes the universal stage, and the curtain the darkness that follows the light. The other of these poems is the rondeau closing the series:

What is to come we know not. But we know
That what has been was good—was good to show,
Better to hide, and best of all to bear,
We are masters of the days that were.
We have lived, we have loved, we have suffered—
even so.

Shall we not take the ebb who had the flow?
Life was our friend. Now, if it be our foe—

Dear, though it spoil and break us!—need we care
　　　What is to come?

Let the great winds their worst and wildest blow,
Or the gold weather round us mellow slow:
We have fulfilled ourselves and we can dare
And we can conquer, though we may not share
In the rich quiet of the afterglow
　　　What is to come.

This is the most personal of the poems in *Bric-à-brac* and the one most indicative of Henley's mature poetic achievement. A love lyric to Anna, it conveys with admirable restraint the sentiment that the individual finds in mutual sympathy his strongest bulwark against the assaults of time and circumstance. And the chosen form is the inevitable vehicle for the expression of that sentiment. As a rondeau, it can be compared in depth and finish only to such pieces as "In After Days" and "In Flanders Fields." It is more than a mere technical tour de force; it represents the poet's attitude towards his world.

Of the formalists, Dobson alone remained consistently faithful to the ballade, the rondeau, and the triolet.[11] Lang and Gosse, having proven their dexterity, returned to less "exotic" couplets and quatrains, wherein they continued to show themselves good honest men, but no poets. Henley who had in him a stronger creative talent than any of these sought an ampler medium of expression. He began to experiment with the free rhythms in which he was later to embody his Whistlerian visions of the London night.

The origins of Henley's "free verse" are difficult to trace. We can seize upon no single book comparable to Banville's *Petit Traité* as the avowed source of technical

[11] From the beginning Dobson wrote much verse in looser rhymed stanzas; but until the end his formal verse represented his best effort. By the time of his death in 1921, his ballades and rondeaus had become standard models for younger poets, especially in America, anxious in an age of *vers libre* occasionally to achieve the discipline of metre.

inspiration. Long since accustomed to neo-Georgian *vers libre*, we do not think to question the form of the poignant "*I. M. Margaritae Sororis*":

> A late lark twitters from the quiet skies;
> And from the west,
> Where the sun, his day's work ended,
> Lingers as in content,
> There falls on the old, gray city
> An influence luminous and serene,
> A shining peace.
>
> The smoke ascends
> In a rosy-and-golden haze. The spires
> Shine, and are changed. In the valley
> Shadows rise. The lark sings on. The sun,
> Closing his benediction,
> Sinks, and the darkening air
> Thrills with a sense of the triumphing night—
> Night with her train of stars
> And her great gift of sleep.
>
> So be my passing!
> My task accomplished and the long day done,
> My wages taken, and in my heart
> Some late lark singing,
> Let me be gathered to the quiet west,
> The sundown splendid and serene,
> Death.

Yet in the 1870's this form was quite as much an innovation as the pattern of Henley's first "*Ballade à double refrain.*" There was little else like it in English; it was less regular than the loosened metres of "The Strayed Reveller," which Arnold appears to have adapted from the mixed iambs and trochees of Goethe's "Prometheus"; and its cadences bore scant resemblance to the oceanic roll of Walt Whitman or the tedious, unscannable "buzz-buzz" of Martin Tupper. Its only structural analogy in nineteenth century poetry is, I believe, to be found in the descriptive passages of Heine's *Nordsee*.[12]

Though Henley knew far less of German literature than of French, he was yet sufficiently familiar with the writings of Heine to contribute an essay on the subject to *Vanity Fair*. Apparently he had read Heine's shorter lyrics in hospital; for, as early as the summer of 1875, he was imitating their broken romanticism:

> The sands are alive with sunshine,
> The bathers lounge and throng,
> And out in the bay a bugle
> Is lilting a gallant song. . . .
>
> While the children romp in the surges,
> And sweethearts wander free,
> And the Firth as with laughter dimples . . .
> I would it were deep over me!

If the shock in the last line of this poem strikes the English reader as too deliberately conceived, it yet indicates a full understanding of the principle of *Stimmungsbrechung* which Henley could likely have learned only from the German poet. Besides such stylistic derivation, there are also in Henley's work a few possible echoes of Heine's verse. The concept of the hospital "mattress-life" probably stems from the section concerning the *Matratzengruft* appended to the *Romanzero*. And a line from the "Ballade of Dead Actors,"

> The curtain falls, the play is played,

may well translate the first line to the eighteenth section of "Lazarus,"

> *Der Vorhang fällt, das Stück ist aus.*

These "borrowings" are, of course, highly debatable and, it may be, quite far-fetched. But the metrical similarity of Henley's verse to the *Nordsee* poems seems to me

[12] *Cf.* Henley's poem with the movement of *"Untergang der Sonne."* Many of Henley's *Rhymes and Rhythms*, see below, p. 188f., read like translations of the *Nordsee*.

more than coincidental.[13] In the matter of *free* verse, I
would not suggest exact parallels between the work of
the one poet and that of the other; for every free poem
by definition must be a law unto itself; it must create
its own tempo. Nonetheless, both poets share the general tendency to make free cadences depend for their
effect upon the rapid recurrence of heavy syllables; both
rely on the sonorous epithet as a means of strong in-
tonation.

To Henley, as to Heine, free verse was a poetic medium not less exacting of the craftsman than more conventional forms. His painstaking revisions of the Hospital sequence will serve to dispel any notion that
irregular metrics may have meant a sacrifice of disciplined technique. The "Vigil," for instance, which might
appear too painfully subjective to admit of alteration,
has suffered a sea-change in the short interval between
the 1887 "Hospital Sketches" and the 1888 *In Hospital*;
subtle mutations in assonance have deepened the plaintive music; shifts in accent have reinforced the insistent
trochaic pattern; added images have realized the dreary
setting in more concrete detail. So, throughout the
whole sequence, the process of addition, subtraction,
transposition continues until the poet has found the
rhythm and the figure that will best evoke the desired
impression. Slowly the memory of personal suffering is
transmuted into the objective hospital drama. Within
the free metres, no single syllable falls inadvertently;
each contributes to the larger architecture of the poem.

In most of his earlier poetry Henley remained the ex-
perimentalist concerned with the problem of technique.
But by 1888, when he gathered *In Hospital, Bric-à-brac*,
and the *Echoes* into his *Book of Verses*, he had so far
solved this problem that the reviewers of his volume
devoted much more space to a discussion of content
than of form. The *Critic* wondered how one who wore

[13] *Cf.* the unrhymed regular trochaic poems like "Waiting" and
"Operation" as to movement with the *"Meeresstille."*

93

the "Gallic bonds" with such ease could be guilty of the Hospital realism, wherein "a French painter of anatomy and vivisection might find a letter-text for illustration." The *Athenaeum* raised the whole question of the propriety of "a realism that is something more than Pre-Raphaelite." Mr. Henley, it went on, was assuredly original in his selection of subject-matter; but "mere originality . . . is not so much the note of the true poet as is often assumed. Otherwise Donne would have to be set beside Tennyson." With regard to form, it would suffice to warn Mr. Henley against "caricatures of Bible rhythm —that divine movement compared with which even the music of Shakespeare and Milton seems almost jejune." Writing in the *Academy*, Cosmo Monkhouse was likewise a little perturbed by the passages of realism; he preferred the more romantic *Echoes*, though he conceded that the theme of *In Hospital* could not have been treated "so effectively in prose." Alice Meynell, on the other hand, lauded Henley's realism, which "told the truth with a direct intention," and discounted the *Echoes*, where "a more or less romantic humour [fitted] less perfectly his beautiful sincerity of expression."[14] The *Saturday Review* agreed that the realism was probably justified:

> Speaking generally, we are no partisans of the realistic method in literature or its products; but the hospital division of Mr. Henley's work constitutes to our minds as interesting a little chapter of realism as is to be found in English poetry since the days of Crabbe.

St. James's Gazette was thankful that Mr. Henley in the Hospital pieces had "kept to the intellectual and emotional side of that which he [had] chosen to deal with, never doing more than touch on the purely physical horrors." More enthusiastic in its appraisal, the *New Princeton Review* saw in the *Book of Verses* "a real addition to the poetry of the day by one who furnishes ample evidence of the true poetic gift"; but, said the anony-

[14] Alice Meynell, *Merry England*, xi (1888), 93, 95.

mous critic, it might "not be out of place to urge Mr. Henley to make the philosophy of his next verses more cheerful."

Insofar as Henley's *Book of Verses* stood at the culmination of a ten-year search for style, the aesthetic element in it was perhaps more pronounced than the strain of realism. Yet only one of the many reviews recognized the poet as a conscious craftsman; and this came from the leader of the aesthetes himself. In the *Woman's World*, Oscar Wilde wrote a notice designed to make Henley "roar like the Bull of Bashan."[15] The Hospital poems were, he admitted, undoubtedly powerful, though they were "still in the twilight, . . preludes, experiments, inspired jottings in a notebook." Here and there among the other verses were strewn "felicitous phrases" and "fanciful lines"; even "the green sky's minor thirds" seemed "perfectly right in its place, and a very refreshing bit of affectation in a volume where there is so much that is natural." The book as a whole testified to the author's exuberance, virility, and sanity— "and sane poets are as rare as blue lilies, though they may not be quite as delightful." From the singer's joy of living, from his "frank delight in experience for its own sake" came "all the faults and all the beauties" of his verse; yet the faults were "deliberate, and the result of much study," while the beauties had "the air of fascinating impromptus." Indeed, if Mr. Henley "took himself more seriously, his work would become trivial."

Despite its calculated cleverness, Wilde's review struck deeper than all others. It suggested the conflict in Henley between the man of action and the man of art; and it related Henley the poet, by virtue of his refreshing affectations and his deliberate style, to the aesthetic group whom Henley the critic so roundly denounced. In it Wilde for the first time crossed swords with the writer who most vigorously would contest his position in the literary life of the 'nineties.

[15] Wilde, quoted by Stuart Mason, *Bibliography of Oscar Wilde* (London, 1914), p. 223.

✎§ CHAPTER 7. COLLABORATION.
THE HENLEY-STEVENSON PLAYS: 1879-1885

HENLEY's essays in formal poetry and free verse represented but one expression of his creative talent during the years of apprenticeship. In the decade that elapsed between the founding of *London* and the launching of the *Scots Observer*, the poet made his bid, valiant though vain, for recognition as a dramatist. Once more his inspiration came from France; he had read widely in the plays of Alfred de Musset and the elder Dumas; he had studied the stagecraft of Augier and Sardou and Labiche; he had weighed the *pièce bien faite* of Scribe against the hack-work of Tom Taylor. Impatient with the Victorian theater, he discovered or encouraged in Louis a like dissatisfaction and a like will to remedy the defect. Accordingly, with all the self-conscious deliberation of a new French school, the two friends organized their revolt. Together, they decided, they might bring Art to the English playhouse. It would be the avowed purpose of their collaboration "to re-create the Romantic Drama in terms of prose."[1]

Years before the writing of *Dr. Jekyll and Mr. Hyde*, Stevenson had been fascinated by the problem of dual personality; at the age of fifteen, he had sketched a play concerning the double life of Deacon Brodie, master carpenter and notorious housebreaker of eighteenth century Edinburgh. This fragment of *juvenilia* lay forgotten till the autumn of 1878 when Henley read the manuscript among Stevenson's papers, made allowance for the execution, and applauded the theme. Entirely rewritten, the *Deacon* might provide an admirable role for Henry Irving, who was at the time proving his abilities as the interpreter of psychological melodrama. The collaborators, therefore, set to work, brimming with enthusiasm and overflowing with theory. By January

---

[1] Henley, *Pall Mall Magazine*, xxv (1901), 513.

they had completed four acts and, while debating the tremendous fifth, had begun a second play. In a joint letter to Colvin, their critical advisor, they explained their practice and their conception of dramatic art; it might be possible, they thought, to transpose a few scenes, but "the act must progress in emotion, not in time. . . . Remember, a play is emotion as a statue is marble. Incident, story, these are but the pedestal." Colvin's criticisms were probably more apposite than the authors would admit; for Irving, on a consideration of the four acts, regretfully declined the whole play.[2] But neither Stevenson nor Henley was to be disheartened by Irving's judgment. If one actor did not appreciate their artistry, another was more sympathetic; "Teddy" Henley, then eighteen years old, "would learn the speeches as fast as they were written," and declaim them with true romantic gusto.[3] In March the *Deacon* was completed; and the playwrights, feverishly excited, talked till dawn of their achievement.[4]

Many plays were planned to follow *Deacon Brodie*. In the impetuosity of the "R. L. S." *post mortem*, Henley lingered affectionately over some of their names: *Ajax, Don Juan, Farmer George, The Tragedy of Hester Noble, The Mother-in-Law, Honour and Arms*, and *Madame Destiny*. But none of these progressed far beyond its "canorous and inspiriting title."[5] Two months after the completion of the *Deacon*, Louis was off to Paris. And in the summer his restless spirit drove him farther afield; defying family and friends, he followed Mrs. Osbourne to California. Henley remained behind in London, the struggling journalist, forced for the time being to forego his ambitions as the author of serious drama.

From America Stevenson wrote agonized letters begging Henley, who was serving as his literary agent, to

[2] See Lucas, *The Colvins*, pp. 108, 113.
[3] See *New York Dramatic Mirror*, xxxv (1896), 2.
[4] See Masson, *Stevenson*, p. 173.   [5] Henley, *PMM*, xxv, 512.

be less severe in his criticisms. His fiction was to be measured against his earlier stories, and not against the best of Fielding or Balzac or even Wilkie Collins. Impoverished, broken in health, he urged his friend to sell whatever he could at whatever price he might obtain. Art could not be his first consideration as long as cash was his prime necessity. For the present, he would have to abandon all hope of continuing collaboration in the drama; plays were much too slowly made; "and understand me, I have to get money *soon*, or it has no further interest for me; I am nearly through my capital."[6] Henley was alarmed not less by the fact that Louis's work had noticeably fallen off than by the fear that Louis himself might be suffering actual want. "Being too blasphemously given towards California and California things" to trust himself to paper, he asked Colvin to write for him, since it was essential "that he should be brought to see that England and a quiet life are what he wants and must have if he means to make—I won't say reputation—but money by literature."[7] Louis, however, did not come back until September, 1880, when he could bring with him his American bride. In describing to Henley his meeting with the couple at Liverpool, Colvin said that he doubted whether he would ever be able to get used "to the little determined brown face and white teeth and grizzling (for that's what it's up to) grizzling hair," which they were henceforth to see at their friend's side.[8] If in due course Colvin did reconcile himself to Mrs. R. L. S., her genteel behavior was to Henley a source of never-ending irritation. Yet it meant much to him to have Louis in England again, even under conditions that would forbid the old intimacy. Henley's thoughts turned once more to the re-creation of the romantic drama in terms of prose.

Privately printed in 1880, *Deacon Brodie* was the first

---

[6] Stevenson, *Works*, xxvii, 127.
[7] Henley, quoted by Lucas, *The Colvins*, pp. 116-17.
[8] See Lucas, p. 128.

book to bear Henley's name upon its title page. And, though no producer could be found so rash as to stage the play, the mere physical reality of the volume gave impetus to Henley's enthusiasm. We find him, a few months later, telling Colvin that he has met the Irish actor, Shiel Barry, and has decided to keep him in mind as the ideal "lead" for *The King of Clubs*, upon which the collaborators were then working; "and I feel sure that if I do not die, and can only get fairly on to the drama, I shall make him a part in which he'll be the talk of London."[9] Louis, on the other hand, was less sanguine; he was far from satisfied with the *Deacon*, and he soon lost interest in *The King of Clubs*. He was increasingly preoccupied with his essays and his novels. Yet in the midst of his non-dramatic prose, the image of Henley was constantly before him. To Henley he dedicated the collected papers *Virginibus Puerisque* in the spring of 1881. Henley became Burly of *Talk and Talkers*, a roaring, "boisterous and piratic" speaker who underwent "passions of revolt and agony," a man "whose presence could be felt in a room you entered blindfold." Above all, Henley inspired his portrait of Long John Silver in *Treasure Island*, as Louis himself confessed in a letter of May, 1883, from Hyères: "It was the sight of your maimed strength and masterfulness that begot John Silver. . . . Of course, he is not in any other quality or feature the least like you; but the idea of the maimed man, ruling and dreaded by the sound, was entirely taken from you."[10]

This "confession" was subscribed "Ever yours, Pretty Sick." And in that odd signature is implicit the real cause of Stevenson's temporary desertion of the drama. Louis was more than "pretty sick"; he felt himself to be dying. "Nobody knew better than he did," said Chesterton, "that nothing is more terrible than a bed; since it is always waiting to be a death-bed." During his illness

9 See Lucas, p. 131.
10 Stevenson, *Works*, xxiii, 316.

at Hyères he wrote his only great poem, the *"Requiem."* Prostrate with pain, attempting to catch the long, moral view of experience, he repudiated Henley's belligerent critical attitude:

> I wish your honesty were not so warfaring. . . . As for these quarrels: in not many years shall we not all be clay-cold and safe below ground, you with your loud-mouthed integrity, I with my fastidious briskness, . . swallowed in silence? It seems to me . . . that when the dustman has gone by, these quarrellings will prick the conscience.[11]

Henley, for his part, was moved to forget his quarrels and to travel southwards. In January, 1884, he passed a week with Louis at Hyères, until the invalid, regaining strength, could accompany him to Nice.

By the spring following Henley's visit, Stevenson had sufficiently recovered to chide him for not having written oftener and at greater length:

> All men are rot, but there are two—
> Sidney, the oblivious Slade, and you—
> Who from the rabble stand confest
> Ten million times the rottenest.
>
> R. L. S.[12]

In July he was moved to England, just too late to share in what had promised to be Henley's triumph. On the second day of that month, *Deacon Brodie* had its London *première* at the old Prince's Theatre with "Teddy" Henley in the title role. Louis had sent Henley his congratulations and had told the "Dear Boy" of his disappointment at missing the performance. But a few days afterwards he admitted to Colvin that the play was "damned bad"—it was to be hoped that his collaborator had not lost too much money on its production. Yet to Henley the *Deacon* was by no means a failure; and a few favorable criticisms among many adverse ones con-

11 Stevenson, *Works*, xxvii, 184-85.
12 *Works*, xxvii, 187.

vinced him that it was a major, if not a universally popular, success. In the autumn he carried his enthusiasm to Bournemouth where he and Anna passed two months with the Stevensons. Here he collaborated with Louis on two new plays, *Beau Austin* and *Admiral Guinea*, written and revised before his return to London. At the end of the year Mrs. R. L. S. wrote Colvin of her husband's poor health—his mother had given him "a dreadful cold"—and suggested to him that Henley might resume his work at Bournemouth—"he might as well bring his influenza here, and join us, as he can do no harm."[13] This was at best a chilly invitation from a woman who had but little respect for Henley and none at all for the plays,[14] who resented the boisterous and piratic man's assuming domination of her well-ordered household, and who considered the dramatic works, which were obviously a financial failure, an unnecessary drain upon Louis's energies and resources. Accordingly, when Henley installed himself at "Skerryvore" in order to write *Macaire*, she made it clear to Louis that his friend was a "wearing" and ill-mannered companion. What with Henley—she told Colvin—and Henley's actorbrother and "Bob" Stevenson and "Bob's" sister and Sargent and Baxter and William Archer, all in her house, she "quite broke down under the strain"; her one solace was "the dear Henry James" who "through it all . . . remained faithful, though he suffered bitterly and openly."[15] Whether at her request or of his own accord, Stevenson discouraged Henley's projects for further collaboration. *Macaire* was the last and wittiest of the plays. After its composition Henley returned to journalism,[16]

[13] See Lucas, pp. 159-60.

[14] See Steuart, *Stevenson*, II, 58-60; and *cf*. Lucas, p. 107.

[15] See Lucas, pp. 166-67.

[16] In addition to the plays in collaboration, Henley, working alone, wrote a farce, *Mephisto*, never published, but produced at the Royalty Theatre, June 14, 1886, with "Teddy" Henley in the title role. Apparently *Mephisto* was an unqualified failure. See *New York Dramatic Mirror*, XXXV (1896), 2.

consigning Louis to a long summer of Jamesian gentility.

In a penetrating essay on Alexandre Dumas, Henley compared the freedom and the passion of romantic drama with the deliberate artifice and controlled craftsmanship of Scribe. Dumas, he said, demanded only "four trestles, four boards, two actors, and a passion"; for to him drama was simply "so much emotion in action." To Scribe, on the other hand, drama was "a perpetual *chassé-croisé* at the edge of a precipice, a dance of puppets among swords that might but will not cut"; and a dramatic situation was "a kind of tight-rope to be crossed with ever so much agility and an endless affectation of peril by all his characters in turn." As an appraisal of the two predominant nineteenth century French dramatic techniques, this judgment indicates the conflicting theories to which Henley and Stevenson subjected themselves. If their dramas were intended to be as passionate as those of Dumas, they were executed with all the artful contrivance of Scribe. And insofar as Dumas and Scribe stood at aesthetic antipodes, the plays represented an imperfect synthesis of spontaneous emotion and calculating workmanship.

Interviewed by the *New York Dramatic Mirror* in 1896, "Teddy" Henley declared that *Deacon Brodie*, despite its failure on the American stage, was without question "the best psychological melodrama ever written." If "Teddy's" judgment was obviously prejudiced, it was not totally perverse. As the product of two young imaginations, the *Deacon* relates itself not to the sentimental intrigues of the mid-Victorian theater, but rather to the splendid bombast of such greater pieces as *Die Räuber* or *Hernani*. Like Schiller's Karl, Brodie turns to crime through none of the stock villain's innate rottenness; his sin is a deliberate protest against a Philistine environment. In the chiming church bells he hears "the trumpets of respectability, sounding encouragement to

102

the world to do and spare not, and not to be found out."
His own hypocrisy is more heroic; as he slips unnoticed
from the locked bedroom, he rationalizes his conduct
in dashing soliloquy: "Trysts are keeping, bottles crack-
ing, knives are stripping; and here is Deacon Brodie
flaming forth the man of men he is!" At Mother Clarke's
he plays Prince Hal in search of a Falstaff with whom
to match wits; his sprightliness of fancy would alone
give him entree into the brilliant and bibulous society
of Eastcheap. He turns a neat epigram: "What! shall we
have no more honour among thieves than there is honesty among politicians?" And he rises buoyantly to sat-
irize the English Captain Rivers: "O Captain! . . There's
nothing like your Englishman for genuine distinction.
He is nearer France than we are, and smells of his neigh-
bourhood." Dialogue so lively does not ill become the
comic interlude; for comedy thrives upon heightened
verbal effects. But the play as a whole is a tragedy; and
in its more sombre scenes, such conscious overwriting
rings hollow; false rhetoric tears its deepest passion to
tatters.

On its serious side, *Deacon Brodie* attempts a study
of the decline and fall of a strong-willed activist hero.
Like the Giaour in his proud confession, the Deacon
half-admires his own intrepidity. And his real defeat
strikes home not through remorse of conscience but
rather through a sense of humiliation at the hands of
the shoddy villain Moore. His power has gone when he
must argue with his lieutenant: "I'm the Deacon, am I
not? . . . And you think to steal a march upon a man
like me? . . . I read your thoughts like print." His
tragedy is the plight of the will that has lost its independence, for ultimately his free decision is overruled
by the clutch of circumstance. Returning from his last
robbery and the murder of his traitorous henchman, he is
confident that his locked bedroom door will provide the
certain alibi. But the door is no longer fastened; the doctor has forced it open to summon him to the bedside of

103

his dying father. Brodie loses complete self-possession as he recognizes the fearful reality. The following dialogue with his sister is dramatically worth the entire play:

> MARY: My father is dead. O, Will, where have you been?
>
> BRODIE: Your father is dead. O yes! He's dead, is he? Dead. Quite right. . . . How did you open the door? It's strange. I bolted it.
>
> M: We could not help it, Will, now could we? The doctor forced it. He had to, had he not?
>
> B: The doctor forced it? The doctor? Was he here? He forced it? He?
>
> M: We did it for the best; it was I who did it . . . I, your own sister. And, O Will, my Willie, where have you been? You have not been in any harm, any danger?
>
> B: Danger? O my young lady, you have taken care of that. It's not danger now, it's death. Death? Ah! Death! Death! Death! . . . Death? Did you say my father was dead? My father? O my God, my poor old father! Is he dead, Mary? Have I lost him? Is he gone? O, Mary dear, and to think of where his son was!

Fear drives Brodie into self-betrayal; all passion spent, he renounces the will to live. But in death itself, his old Byronic pride quickens briefly once again. Scorning the ignominy of suicide or of capture, he grasps his hanger and lunges towards the detective "who parries and runs him through." His dying lips invoke "the new life. . . the new life!"

The work of a poet and a novelist, *Deacon Brodie* is literary rather than dramatic in its appeal and in its merits. Again and again the dialogue serves merely as a prelude to the monologue. Brodie in company exercises a sharp wit; but he remains an intellectual figment, seldom realized in human terms. Brodie *solus*, on the other hand, becomes a creature of passion; and his speech approaches lyricism. The soliloquies fall almost too easily into the iambic rhythms of blank verse, as if the playwrights were impatient with the prose medium. These are the best portions of the play. Yet they have no direct relation to the movement of the whole; they describe an emotion which never collides with a comparable rival emotion. Even the romantic Dumas demanded *two* actors; for it takes more than one swallow to make a summer, and more than one character to make a play. But the Deacon stands alone; his conflict is scarcely more tangible than Manfred's; and his poetic cries are, therefore, of no greater consequence.

What is true of *Deacon Brodie* is largely true of the three later plays, though none attains the *Deacon's* intensity of theme. *Admiral Guinea*, the most serious of these, concerns a reformed slave-trader's opposition to his daughter's marriage with a carefree young sailor. Blind Pew, fresh from *Treasure Island*, serves unconsciously as the *deus ex machina*; for it is only through a thwarting of Pew's attempt at robbery that the youth may win the approval of the pharisaical Captain Gaunt. Bernard Shaw thought the melodrama a "frankly boyish compound of piracy and pasteboard, coming occasionally very close to poetry and pasteboard," but recognized behind it a "prodigious literary virtuosity" and a genuine sense of stagecraft.[17] And William Archer was so much impressed by the poetry that he was inclined to ignore the pasteboard; its literary quality, he felt, was undeniable; the Admiral spoke "a prose no more to be tampered with than the most delicate verse"; and Pew touched "the sublime of scoundrelism," repeatedly proving himself "the master of his fate, the captain of his soul."[18] We would agree with Shaw that some of the stage effects are well engineered; the entrance of the blind man, intent upon robbery, who imagines himself detected by the sleepwalking Admiral, occasions a truly

[17] See George Bernard Shaw, *Our Theatres in the Nineties* (London, 1932), III, 263-64.

[18] See William Archer, *The Theatrical World of 1897* (London, 1898), pp. 320, 322, 324, 338.

dramatic situation. Nor would we dissent from Archer's praise of Pew; for from the rogue's first appearance we are face to face with a full-blown, cheerful liar of amazing vivacity:

> Good Christian lady, help a poor blind mariner to a mouthful of meat. I've served His Majesty in every quarter of the globe; I've spoke with 'Awke and glorious Anson, as I might with you; and I've tramped it all night long, upon my sinful feet, and with an empty belly.

But not even Pew can enrich *Admiral Guinea's* poverty of theme. The titular hero, for all his eloquence, is a hollow man, a mere peg whereon to hang a superficial tirade against the same false morality that Stevenson rebuked in "A Christmas Sermon." His final curtain speech reinforces the essentially juvenile message of the play; as he looks upon the dead pirate, he muses:

> But for the grace of God, there lies John Gaunt! Christopher, you have saved my child; and I, I, that was blinded with self-righteousness, have fallen. Take her, Christopher; but O, walk humbly.

This is no more convincing as a study of repentance than the conclusion of Kingsley's *Two Years Ago*, which on the whole presents a much clearer picture of the will in defeat. Thus, despite a stagecraft worthy at times of Scribe himself, *Admiral Guinea*, like *Deacon Brodie*, has but a passive value; it survives not as a living art, but rather as the amateur's attempt to achieve drama through mere "literary virtuosity."

The literary flavor of the Henley-Stevenson plays proves more palatable in *Beau Austin* than in the melodramas; for *Beau Austin*, designed and executed as a high comedy of manners, naturally relates itself to an urbane cultural tradition. When produced by Beerbohm Tree at the Haymarket Theatre in November, 1890, it became the theatrical event of the season; in exemplifying the "artistic good-breeding" of Dobson's society verse, it made its distinct appeal to a cultivated West

106

End audience. Henley's "Prologue" in conventional couplets decorously introduced the theme:

"To all and singular," as Dryden says,
We bring a fancy of those Georgian days,
Whose style still breathed a faint and fine perfume
Of old-world courtliness and old-world bloom. . . .

By the authors' explicit direction each of the acts was prefaced by the appropriate musical induction, by airs from Handel and Gluck, by "The Lass of Richmond Hill," and the "Minuet" from *Don Giovanni*. The charm of the piece struck even the fastidious Henry James who described the *première*, in a highly characteristic letter to Stevenson, as "the only honourable affair transacted *dans notre sale tripot* for many a day."[19] The play's remoteness from reality seems to have worried neither James nor the younger critics who, in the suite of Wilde and Whistler, no longer denied the artifice of art.

Beau Austin owes little to Victorian plays on similar themes. Douglas Jerrold's *Beau Nash* is merely an expanded anecdote of a shabby-genteel gamester's magnanimity of spirit. And Blanchard Jerrold's *Beau Brummel* grows maudlin over a dandy's pathetic death in the squalor of Caen. *Beau Austin* stems less from these than from the eighteenth century theater wherein witty was the way of the world. Miss Foster, for instance, is an amiable Augustan rationalist who sensibly urges the more squeamish Dorothy to ignore her brother's adolescent escapades. Dorothy, as her aunt characterizes her and as she reveals herself, derives from the sentimental comedy of Steele and his successors. Seduced and abandoned by George Austin, she spares her emotion for interminable agonized soliloquy. Her lover Fenwick, who resembles Faulkland in *The Rivals*, likewise sentimentalizes until his speech becomes a caricature of true passion; and we cannot but feel that the collaborators are at least partly satirical in their attitude towards his

[19] Percy Lubbock, ed., *The Letters of Henry James*, 2 vols. (New York, 1920), i, 176.

107

bombast. The Beau himself descends from both the Congrevian and sentimental comedy-types. He inclines long enough in the direction of sentimentalism to heed the outraged Fenwick's entreaties and humbly to confess his guilt before Dorothy and the Duke of York, when the girl's brother threatens to cause a scene. But when Dorothy succumbs to his humility, romantically calling, "My hero! take me," he straightway recovers his reason and his dignity: "My dear creature, remember that we are in public. . . . Your Royal Highness, may I present you Mrs. George Frederick Austin?" Thus as the curtain falls, good breeding glosses over unseemly emotion. The play closes not with the whines of Fenwick but with the decorum of the gracious gentleman.

When Henry Irving revived the harlequinade *Macaire* at the Lyceum Theatre in May, 1895, Bernard Shaw regretted the actor's selection of an "old third-class version which gave him unlimited scope for absurdity"; the choice was, he said, doubly deplorable at a time when there was available a new and vital version by Henley and Stevenson, "which was full of literary distinction." Apparently heartened by this gratuitous praise, Henley printed the previously unpublished version of *Macaire* in the June issue of his *New Review*. Thereupon Shaw's eulogy continued as a lively attack on the Philistinism of the middle classes, which could scarcely be expected ever to appreciate such "wit, imagination, romance, and humor."[20] And his criticism, based as it was on his own experience with the bourgeois audience, accurately predicted the play's fortunes; for, unlike *Beau Austin*, *Macaire* enjoyed not even a seasonal vogue in the London theater. But whether or not it failed behind the footlights is beside the point. *Macaire* remains the most readable of all the Henley-Stevenson plays, a nimble and engaging farce, a not unworthy antecedent of *The Importance of Being Earnest*.

20 See Shaw, *Our Theatres*, I, 114, 143-44.

108

A prefatory note to *Macaire* suggests that "the time between the acts should be as brief as possible, and the piece played, where it is merely comic, in a vein of patter." This stage direction indicates the authors' attitudes towards their work and the general tone of the play itself. *Macaire* is the shortest and least ambitious product of the dramatic collaborations, and at the same time the most successful. In it the amateur playwrights, relaxed and whimsical, reduce the intricate intrigue of an old French melodrama to a single situation, such as may provide ample opportunity for the exercise of a sharp wit and a changeful humor. Macaire himself presents an amazing complex of intellect and ingenuity. He shares Iago's sense of realism and Mercutio's turn for speculation. And with Bertrand as his Spark, he is not less of the poet than Fantasio. At the wedding he simulates to perfection the hearty joy of Falstaff, as he urges the fiddlers to their catgut and bids the villagers quicken their heels. About to murder the Marquis, he finds inspiration for his deed in Macbeth's "Out, out, brief candle!" On another occasion he echoes Schiller's Talbot with the query: "But what can men or gods against stupidity?" Then again he seems to anticipate the unpredictable Shavians:

> The affections, my lord, are priceless. Money will not buy them; or, at least, it takes a great deal. . . .
> Fool! would I harm a fly, when I had nothing to gain? As the butcher with the sheep, I kill to live; and where is the difference between man and mutton? pride and a tailor's bill. Murder? I know who made that name—a man crouching from the knife! Selfishness made it—the aggregated egotism called society.

The character of Macaire alone dominates the whole farce. But in that character there is no consistency, no humanity, no growth, and no decay. There is nothing tragic in his fatal fall down the staircase that leads from the Marquis's chamber. Death has no commerce with a repentant rogue; death merely checks an almost incredible flow of wit and romance and reason—

> Sold for the last time; at least, the last time this side
> death. Death—what is death?

The failure of the Henley-Stevenson plays on the English stage was less remarkable than the eulogy heaped upon these plays by the keenest dramatic critics of the 'nineties. Shaw and Archer, as we have seen, turned their wrath upon a public which could be blind to artistry so obvious. Allan Monkhouse, who spoke of the "high excellence" of the plays in general, felt sure that *Beau Austin* in particular was "destined to become a classic," insofar as it was "witty almost as Congreve, and with a far better hold on life."[21] And Clement Shorter, in his jubilee survey of Victorian literature, described the same piece as "probably the greatest contribution to the drama of the era." Historically, such judgments are not incomprehensible; for critics familiar with the talents of Wilde, Jones, and Pinero, of the translated Ibsen, and of Shaw himself, could look back upon the 'eighties only as a barren decade, a decade to whose taste the three hundred tearful nights of Buchanan's *Sophia* were sufficient index. In the midst of that desert, Henley and Stevenson stood, a promising but neglected oasis. They alone in an otherwise "aesthetic" period considered drama as an "aesthetic" problem. Though neither of them possessed or understood the dramatic imagination, their collaborated plays yet remained as a serious experiment in style, an inspiration to the greater playwrights of the 'nineties.

21 Allan Monkhouse, *Books and Plays* (London, 1894), pp. 187, 189.

110

ی CHAPTER 8. THE CRITIC OF ART. LONDON: 1880-1888

THOUGH dramatic collaboration absorbed much of Henley's time in the 'eighties, the writing of plays was, after all, little more than a diversion from the strenuous round of journalism. While Stevenson, penniless and sick for home, lingered in America awaiting Fanny Osbourne's divorce, Henley continued to eke out his livelihood as occasional reviewer for a half-dozen London papers. Necessity proved the mother of versatility; and he found himself prepared to write with equal ease of politics, music, drama, or literature. But, despite a plethora of hack-work, he lost nothing of his warm enthusiasms. When he attended the exhibition of a Millet painting in April, 1880, he grew almost incoherent from sheer excitement. "I saw it," he told Colvin,

> I saw it. O Colvin, Colvin! Why will you not make an art-critic of me? I am not a bloody fool, for I can feel and see and be religious over great art. We went and looked through the Grosvenor afterwards, and Lord! how poor it all seemed! Beside that solemn fateful figure, those mysterious birds, that fatidic landscape, that prophet's tree. . . .[1]

In the following year, though not yet established as an art-critic, he was given the opportunity of making explicit his appreciation of the French master; to the Fine Art Society's album of Millet reproductions, he contributed a critical introduction, in which he compared the modern painter not unfavorably to Michelangelo. Infuriated by the odious comparison and enraged by Henley's general estimate of the French romantic movement, John Ruskin called public attention to the essay in an article on the immorality of contemporary fiction, which appeared in the *Nineteenth Century* for October, 1881. But Ruskin's absolutism no

[1] Quoted by Lucas, *The Colvins*, p. 122.

111

longer commanded unqualified respect; for 1881 was the year of *Patience*, and London was more concerned with half-ludicrous "aesthetic" young men than with solemn mid-Victorian prophets. Henley himself was something of Gilbert's Heavy Dragoon in whom a swaggering force went hand in hand with "the grace of an Odalisque." If his self-assurance resembled at times the temerity of Lord Waterford, his "keen penetration" was indisputable. He was at once the most vigorous and the most sensitive of the younger critics. His voice, therefore, was heard above the lament of the patriarch. In the month of Ruskin's attack, he accepted the editorship of the *Magazine of Art*, to which he was fully resolved "to introduce a new régime." J. M. Robertson, however, with whom he discussed his ambitious plan, questioned the possibility of its accomplishment; "I have a notion," Robertson wrote to Archer, "he'll ruin the *Magazine* in six months, if he doesn't get sacked in three. He is much too good for the place, I should say."[2] Eventually his prediction proved sound; Henley who preferred critical excellence to popular appeal collided repeatedly with his publishers, until, disgusted beyond reconciliation, he resigned his post. But the final break came only after painful labors and long deliberation. For nearly five years he remained at the helm; and in that time he exerted a distinct influence on the development of English taste.

The first issue of the *Magazine of Art* under Henley's direction convinced Colvin that his friend's self-confidence was well warranted; "Hooray for the mag.," he shouted, "it's a first-rate [one] and the firm is an ungrateful firm if it don't vote a testimonial of several thousand pounds and an épergne to the editor."[3] Coming from the Slade Professor of Art at Cambridge, this was high praise indeed. And yet it was praise not unmerited. For Henley from the outset of his undertaking dis-

2 Quoted by C. Archer, *Wm. Archer*, p. 94.
3 See Lucas, p. 133.

played the editorial brilliance that was to secure for him a dominant place in the literary life of the 'nineties. In the matter of contributors alone, the *Magazine* was a remarkable achievement. Month after month it carried the writings of critics so competent as George Saintsbury, Francis Watt, Edward Tyas Cook, William Archer, Brander Matthews, and Cosmo Monkhouse. In its pages Austin Dobson explained the realism and the satire of Hogarth; David Hannay wrote lively descriptions of the structure of clipper ships; Andrew Lang with whimsical erudition told of Japanese bogies and their place in art; and "Bob" Stevenson made his debut as student of the Barbizon School. From time to time Louis submitted prose pieces and many of the delightful quatrains later to be included in *A Child's Garden of Verses*. Henley, who encouraged all of these able writers, was himself more prolific than any. Taking all art to be his province, he placed his own initials after essays on a wide variety of aesthetic subjects; he made effortless transitions from a discussion of "Medals of the Stage" to a survey of "Some Japanese Painters," from an appraisal of "Two Busts of Victor Hugo" to "A Gossip about the Paris Opera." In addition, he wrote unsigned notes to accompany innumerable frontispieces and full-page illustrations, notes that betrayed an understanding of every school and every technique. Yet his very range of interest might have meant a superficiality of appreciation; and his mere amplitude of vision might have implied a lack of principle. The fact that his criticism attained power as well as breadth testified to the firmness of the conviction behind it. Nor were his standards of judgment entirely subjective in origin or arbitrary in direction. They arose from a deep familiarity with the aesthetic temper of the age; and they bore a timely relevance to contemporary creative methods and critical tendencies.

Aesthetically as well as intellectually, the 'seventies marked a cleavage between early Victorian ideals and late. At the beginning of the decade, Buchanan had

113

sensed the rise of a new and fleshly art; by the end, Whistler's vindication in the Grosvenor trial stood as a symbol of the passing of an older "moral" aesthetic. In 1846 George Darley had seen the day at hand when painting would sink "into a mere ancillary condition, into an aid towards the greater end—Civilization."[4] In 1884 George Frederick Watts complained that contemporary painting served no purpose at all, since men no longer believed "in Art as an agent in real civilisation."[5] But the condition that Watts lamented seemed to Whistler the only condition under which true painting could thrive; the *Ten O'Clock* declared that great art must exist as a self-dependent unit, freed from foreign entanglements, heedless of any end beyond itself, "reticent of habit, abjuring all obtrusiveness, purposing in no way to better others." Henley was more than aware of these conflicting ideologies; as editor of an art journal, he felt it incumbent upon him to take sides. Though he denied sympathy with the affectation of the Wildean aesthetes, he professed belief in the autonomy of the artist. He consistently championed the work of Whistler; and he described the "enchanting *Ten o'Clock*" as "an indigestion of strawberries, a feast for the high Gods, which I fear . . . has not had anything like the effect to which its art and brilliancy, let alone its rightness, entitle it." Of the "moral" art-critic, he spoke disparagingly: "Ruskin . . . uplifted a most beautiful voice, and tenored nonsense, nonsense, for many years and through interminable volumes."[6] It scarcely troubled Henley that in his own literary reviews he insisted not less than Ruskin on the social function of the poet and novelist. For literature, he argued, dealt naturally in ideas of moral and intellectual significance, while painting relied

[4] Darley, quoted by Claude Colleer Abbott, *The Life and Letters of George Darley* (Oxford, 1928), p. 171.

[5] Watts, quoted by M. S. Watts, *George Frederick Watts*, 2 vols. (London, 1912), ii, 37.

[6] *Works*, iv, 364-65.

for its effects on line and color, arranged in suggestive design, but subject to no particular ethical connotation.

Henley's distinction between literary and graphic art served as an invaluable antidote to misapplied Ruskinism. *Modern Painters* had merely urged a singleness of "moral" purpose in all the creative arts. But the Pre-Raphaelites, whose careful craftsmanship Ruskin commended, strove to attain a unity of aesthetic effect; deliberately they confused the diverse media of artistic expression. In the hands of Rossetti a poem frequently developed into a word-painting; and a picture became a detailed transcript of such visual objects as had the value of poetic symbolism. Henley misconstrued Ruskin's theory, and dismissed it summarily as unworthy of serious consideration. But he understood and evaluated Pre-Raphaelite practice; and to an attack on its influence he devoted much time and energy. Like Whistler, he raised strenuous objection to a naïve acceptance of the "truth-to-nature" ideal:

> To render the facts . . . grain by grain, or hair by hair, or petal by petal, is to play a losing game with the camera. Imitation for its own sake is the basest of aims, and the pursuit of it can have but the meanest results.[7]

This implied a direct condemnation of pictures like Holman Hunt's "Scapegoat," wherein the animal was transcribed to the canvas literally "hair by hair." The Pre-Raphaelite, to be sure, might deny interest in "imitation for its own sake," by maintaining the story-value of his factual matter. "The Scapegoat," for instance, was obviously intended to embody a complete parable relative to the lost human soul; and "Cophetua and the Beggar Maid" was designed to evoke a whole familiar legend through its exactitude of detail. To Henley, however, the "realism" with a narrative dimension beyond itself was far more repugnant than the merely self-sufficient literalism; Holman Hunt was a greater offender than

[7] *Works*, IV, 292.

Nasmyth; and Burne-Jones's was a more insidious influence than W. P. Frith's. While the literalists were simply uninspired, the story-telling Pre-Raphaelites were guilty of an attempt self-consciously to pervert the pictorial medium:

> The "Aesthetic Movement" has made painting so excessively literary, that it is either literature in a new medium or it is nothing. But the literature is not for the crowd: it is high-romantic, old-world, mystical; and with the crowd, which loves incident, and is interested in character, it passes for painting.[8]

Even Landseer, who was "essentially popular and . . . mostly innocent of style," was far more cognizant than the aesthetes of the true meaning of art; he was "by no means blind to the fact that to exist as an arrangement in paint is a picture's first condition of excellence." The great graphic artists were those who had best mastered their medium, who had learned to express their individuality within the conventions of the genre. Corot was pre-eminent in his generation, because he most fully knew "that enjoyment of his medium for its own sake denied—they tell us—even to Raphael; his sense of colour was infallibly distinguished and refined; his treatment of the rarest type." Likewise, Delacroix, despite "the violence, the brutality, the insincerity, the bad taste" which were the attributes of his romantic Muse, achieved distinction, insofar as he recognized and accepted the only terms under which genuine painting could subsist; "if he did nothing else, he thought in pictures." The failure so to think in pictures and the consequent confusion of painting with literature led art inevitably "into a state of hopeless anecdotage."[9] It was, therefore, the function of the critic who wished to encourage a vital painting to insist upon a prerequisite understanding of the pictorial medium. He was neither to ask nor to expect the effects of literature from an art operating under

[8] *Works*, IV, 338, n.   [9] *Works*, IV, 250.

different conventions; for "he who reads words into paint is merely a literary person who might be very much better employed."[10] Critics like Sainte-Beuve or R. A. M. Stevenson who judged painting by its own standards endured as sound interpreters; but "the literary critic of art [died] of his own literature."[11] In the preface to his *Views and Reviews: Art*, Henley exculpated himself from any possible charge of "picture-reading"; unlike Ruskin and Hazlitt, he had kept his criticism "more or less unlettered, . . fairly well purged of sentiment," and if like them he had failed, his failure at least was "not on all-fours with theirs." The ideal of unlettered art-criticism made possible Henley's appreciation of the Whistlerian "arrangements"[12] and prepared the way for the English acceptance of the French impressionists who subordinated all literary and character interest to the demands of light and shade. It was an ideal valid in itself and valid in that it exposed to ridicule such purple passages as that in which Walter Pater had described "all the thought and experience of the world" etched upon the countenance of Leonardo's Mona Lisa.

Despite his persistent demand for nonliterary painting, Henley showed a keen interest in the art of illustration. For his journal he reviewed enthusiastically the lithographic work in expensive new printings of *Romeo and Juliet*, Molière's *Théâtre*, Musset's poetry, and the Rabelais saga. Nor did he neglect the inclusion of original black-and-white drawings in the *Magazine* itself. Much of the poetry he published on its large pages was fitted into pen-and-ink marginal designs of the sort that enjoyed a considerable vogue in many late Victorian periodicals. From time to time there would appear the neatly turned verse of Austin Dobson, framed by decorative scrolls and vignettes of Randolph Caldecott. Often

[10] *Works*, IV, 364.   [11] *Works*, IV, 327.

[12] *Cf.* Whistler's explanation of his musical titles as designed to rid his pictures of literary associations, *The Gentle Art of Making Enemies* (London, 1904), pp. 126-28.

the harmony between poem and illustration was so admirably effected that it would have been difficult to decide which of the two had suggested the other. Several of Henley's own lyrics, too fragile to stand as independent units, were apparently conceived as suitable material for the illustrator's craft; the erotic little "Memory," for instance, existed in and for the image about which its stanzas draped themselves, the image of a maiden with a parasol, wandering down a quiet cathedral close.[13] A stronger poem required a less sentimental interpretation; the "Ballade of Dead Actors" gained something of the grotesquerie of Jacobean melodrama from the leering death's-head that accompanied its first publication. Such interplay between the poet's skill and the lithographer's implied no real disavowal of the insistence upon "unlettered" graphic art. A good illustration, Henley maintained, must first of all be a good picture; it must draw from literature the materials of an unliterary design. Charles Keene's work, for instance, had value insofar as it was to be viewed primarily as "a pictorial combination of black-and-white, an effect achieved by certain contrasts of light with dark and line with form," a series of patterns significant in themselves, apart from any verbal context. The successful lithographer, then, was he who, like the true painter, satisfied the conditions of his chosen medium.

Throughout his art-criticism Henley sought to judge by the artist's own standards. A good picture was to be determined by its creator's capacity for design and his power of selection, by his sense of draughtsmanship and his sensitivity to color. A good picture was to be complete in itself. Whereas Ruskin had demanded aspiration of the artist, Henley asked finished expression; to him the "cult of imperfection," which had engendered an admiration for handmade teacups and had inspired the philosophy of Rabbi Ben Ezra, could in nowise supply

[13] See *Magazine of Art*, IX (1886), 385; the illustrator's name, appropriately enough, was J. Fulleylove.

Ballade of Dead Actors.

WHERE are the passions they essayed,
And where the tears they taught to flow?
Where the wild humours they portrayed
For laughing worlds to see and know?
Othello's wrath and Juliet's woe?
Sir Peter's whims and Timon's gall?
And Millamant and Romeo?—
Into the night go one and all!

Where are their braveries fresh or frayed?
The plumes, the armours—friend and foe?
The cloth of gold, the rare brocade?
The mantles glittering to and fro?
The pomp, the pride, the royal show?
The cries of war and festival?
The youth, the grace, the charm, the glow?—
Into the night go one and all.

The curtain falls, the play is played:
The Beggar packs beside the Beau;
The Monarch troops, and troops the Maid;
The Thunder huddles with the Snow.
Where are the revellers, high and low?
The clashing swords? The lovers' call?
The dancers, gleaming row on row?—
Into the night go one and all.

Envoy.

Prince, in one common overthrow,
The hero tumbles with the thrall.
As dust that drives, as straws that blow,
Into the night go one and all.

BALLADE OF DEAD ACTORS
By Elihu Vedder

a stimulus to the fine arts. The time had passed, he said, when "loose drawing" could be "quoted as a characteristic of style, and false colour as a sign of genius." Convinced that the first essential of aesthetic achievement was a strenuously disciplined technique, he would fully have endorsed Stevenson's advice to a scholarship student at the Slade School: "In your own art, bow your head over technique. Think of technique when you rise and when you go to bed. Forget purposes in the meanwhile; get to love technical processes; to glory in technical successes. . . ."[14] Having thoroughly mastered his craft, the artist who would be creative rather than merely imitative, was to strive in all "sincerity" to express his individual talent. If he could find his own style within an established tradition, it ill-behoved him to indulge in novel experiment. If, however, he could discover in the work of others no parallel to his own peculiar gift, he must seek new modes of articulation. By his acceptance of a vital convention, Sir Joshua Reynolds cut "a far more brilliant and conspicuous figure in the art of the world than any Englishman before or since his time." Manet, on the other hand, found no precedent for his unique approach to the mystery of light; and it was, therefore, to his credit that he had the courage to develop the technique and "the theory of what is called *impressionnisme*." Reynolds and Manet were both great artists; for each succeeded in creating, in his own way, but entirely in terms of paint, an atmosphere and a style.

As art-critic, Henley displayed an amazing catholicity of taste. In addition to the innumerable notices published in the *Magazine of Art*, he prepared soundly provocative word-sketches concerning each of the several hundred painters represented at the more important exhibitions of the 'eighties.[15] From all such critical esti-

14 Stevenson, *Works*, xxvii, 175.
15 The art volumes and catalogues that Henley edited or compiled in the 'eighties included: *Millet's Etchings* (London, 1881), *The Graphic*

mates, he gathered fifty-nine succinct appraisals to be reissued in 1901 as the second part of his *Views and Reviews*. Prefaced by a remarkable "Note on Romanticism," this volume indicated his sympathy with many phases of modern art and his particular interest in the French romantic movement. With an almost Marlovian delight in proper names, he catalogued the genius footloose in Paris at the advent of the July Monarchy; breathlessly he listed the caricaturists, comedians, and critics, the historians, musicians, and novelists, the sculptors, lyrists, dramatists, and singers, the lithographers and journalists, of the *annus mirabilis*, 1830. "In the intellectual history of the world," he wrote, "it would, I apprehend, be difficult, if not impossible, to name an epoch in which so many men attained to such eminence in so many of the arts at once. . . . Romanticism brings into action the full orchestra of the arts."

Had the Pre-Raphaelites responded to the manifold stimulus of the French romantics, English painting might never have strayed into the cul de sac of pseudo-medieval artifice. Inasmuch, however, as the culture of France was generally suspect, the Brotherhood failed to recognize the main line of development in modern art passing through the accomplishment of 1830. It was, therefore, the task of the late Victorian critic to recall the painter to a sense of direction. Acutely conscious of his mission, Henley first indicated the vitality of the pre-impressionist French schools as opposed to the lifeless gentility of the Royal Academy. Among English art-critics, he first viewed modern painting in its cosmopolitan context. He was the earliest to appreciate the relation of a landscape artist, misunderstood and neglected in England, to the continental craftsmen; Constable, he said, "foreshadowed a world of possibilities";

Gallery of Shakespeare's Heroines (London, 1888), *Memorial Catalogue of the French and Dutch Loan Collection* (Edinburgh, 1888), *A Century of Artists* (Glasgow, 1889), *Sir Henry Raeburn* (Edinburgh, 1889).

his successes "were the inspiration of what is fast coming to be recognised as the loftiest expression of modern painting; for not far behind them was the art of Rousseau, Daubigny, Dupré, Courbet, Diaz, and, above all, Millet and Corot." In such criticism Henley was deliberately the pioneer, insisting upon the aesthetic use of aesthetic materials, suggesting the evolution of technical processes, widening the horizons of appreciation. By virtue of his essays on Rodin, he was also the prophet, endowed with a sense of historical perspective, able to declare with certainty that here was "sculpture in its essence, sculpture with all its conditions accepted and fulfilled"; however much an insensitive public might ignore him, Rodin already had proven himself: "He is our Michelangelo; and if he had not been that, he might well have been our Donatello."

Messrs. Cassell, who published the *Magazine of Art*, found Henley's bent for prophecy a deterrent to their journal's sales, insofar as it unsettled popular prejudice that it might herald meritorious innovation. Accordingly, they urged upon him a greater orthodoxy of tone and a less iconoclastic editorial policy. Long impatient of all interference, Henley tendered his resignation in August, 1886. A few weeks later he was off with Anna to Paris, "blithe as a great overgrown schoolboy on a holiday jaunt."[16] There at the Hotel Jacob, *rue* Jacob, he played host to Louis and Fanny Stevenson and to Will Low and his many artist friends. Shortly after his arrival he sought out Rodin, whom he had met several years before, and whom he now found anxious to acknowledge the eulogy by which the *Magazine* had lifted his English reputation above his French.[17] As a token of his gratitude Rodin fashioned the bust of Henley later to be placed in replica in the Crypt of St. Paul's. Henley, in turn, held a *déjeuner* in Rodin's honor "at the restau-

16 Will H. Low, *Chronicle of Friendships*, p. 320.
17 See Victor Frisch and J. T. Shipley, *Auguste Rodin* (New York, 1939), p. 117.

rant Lapérouse in the Quai des Grands-Augustins, a re-sort beloved of Voltaire and his associates near the Palais de Justice."[18] It seemed entirely fitting that his career as art-editor should so conclude in animated con-versation with the modern master he most had admired.

Henley's break with his publishers marked the end of his apprenticeship. His refusal to compromise a high critical standard stood as the first complete expression of the fierce independence that would characterize his editorial work of the 'nineties. By 1886 he had estab-lished a reputation and a style; though then and always far from financial security, he no longer doubted his powers of earning a livelihood through journalism. By virtue of his insatiable curiosity, his infinite capacity, his self-assurance, and his energy, he was recognized as an authority on many subjects, highly literate, strongly opinionated, prepared to speak his own mind in his own ringing voice.

After his resignation, two years passed before he found opportunity of reasserting his editorial talents. But in that time he was neither idle nor silent. He saw and judged every aspect of the life about him; and the monthly "London Letters" that he contributed to the New York *Critic* were monuments to his awareness and his range of interests.[19] He continued to excite enthusi-asms and censures as reviewer for the literary weeklies; and he worked with impressive efficiency as compiler of the art anthologies and catalogues. Moreover, it was in this period that he came forward as one of the more promising among the new poets; in 1887 his poems ap-peared prominently in Gleeson White's *Ballades and Rondeaus* and in H. B. Donkin's *Voluntaries for an East London Hospital*; and in the following year David Nutt

18 Low, p. 328.
19 Henley contributed the "London Letter" to the *Critic* from Feb-ruary 27, 1886, to February 4, 1888, over the initials "H. B." A note in the *Critic*, xi (1889), 183, identifies these contributions as Henley's.

published his *Book of Verses*, a little volume whose vigor even Wilde could not but concede.

The interval between editorships brought a close to the intimacy with Stevenson, which necessitated immediate personal adjustment and which later was to affect Henley's general reputation. Throughout the winter of 1886-1887, Henley paid frequent visits to "Skerryvore" where he found Louis, weak of body, mentally exhausted from overwriting, troubled by vague moral compunctions. As the plays were now a dead issue which neither chose to discuss, Henley made other subjects of conversation. He strove to encourage the invalid's interest in music, by strumming upon the piano "The Magic Flute" "with two melodious fingers,"[20] or by shadowing forth some "painful hints of the enormous and distressing suggestiveness which Beethoven expressed into the slow movements of his sonatas."[21] From London he sent Canaletto prints and Piranesi etchings, books, and long letters of literary gossip. But Louis was to be diverted by neither music nor art nor lively conversation. In his suffering he became gloomy, self-reproachful, introspective. Yet by midsummer he had regained something of his old conviviality; one evening in August he seemed "hilariously gay" as he bade farewell to Colvin and Henley.[22] Then the next day, in defiance of his friends' wishes, he left England for the last time.

"For me," said Henley after Louis's death, "there were two Stevensons: the Stevenson who went to America in '87; and the Stevenson who never came back. The first I knew, and loved; the other I lost touch with, and, though I admired him, did not greatly esteem."[23] Henley himself was partly responsible for the final break in the thirteen-year friendship. Tactlessly he wrote to Louis in March, 1888, suggesting plagiarism in one of Fanny Stevenson's short stories; and Louis as impetuously an-

[20] See J. A. Hammerton, *Stevensoniana* (London, 1903), p. 159.
[21] Henley, *PMM*, xxv, 513.   [22] See Steuart, *Stevenson*, ii, 107.
[23] *PMM*, xxv, 506.

ered the charge in virulent letters to Charles Baxter.
___is was ostensibly the beginning of the quarrel. Yet
its roots were deeper than any ill-considered correspondence. In the very circumstances attendant upon
Louis's flight to America were elements sufficient to
arouse Henley's impatience and disgust. Stevenson had
turned his back on London and his London friends; he
had accepted attractive offers from New York publishing houses; he had sold himself to the genteel tradition.[24]
The "old, riotous, intrepid Stevenson" was dead and
buried; and in "the Shorter Catechist of Vailima" who
had appeared to replace him even before the exodus to
Samoa, Henley could have no conceivable interest.

The loss of Stevenson was counterbalanced by the
birth of a daughter, Margaret Emma Henley, on September 4, 1888. Straightway the child became the center
of her father's life, the token that his long struggle
against debt and disease had been meaningful. Ten
weeks after her arrival Henley moved his family north
to Edinburgh, where he was to begin his work as editor
of the newly established *Scots Observer*. There, in the
city that had first given him a measure of health, that
had inspired much of his poetry and had launched him
upon the journalist's career, that had joined him in marriage to Anna, that had laid the scene for his friendship
with Louis and for their first and longest play—there he
entered upon his true maturity. Whatever gods might
be had fitted the tragi-comedy of fifteen years into a
pattern more deeply dramatic than any the collaboration could evolve.

[24] *Cf.* Stevenson's genteel rejection of Henley's favorite author,
Fielding, as "dirty, dull, and false." "Some Gentlemen in Fiction,"
Scribner's Magazine, III (1888), 766.

PART III. "ENGLAND, MY ENGLAND"

What have I done for you,
   England, my England?
What is there I would not do,
   England, my own?

—PRO REGE NOSTRO

◀§ CHAPTER 9. THE MILITANT TORY. THE POLITICAL BIAS: 1888-1901

AWARE that Sidney Colvin loyally supported Gladstone's principles and policies, Henley salted his criticism of the *Landor* with a wry postscript:

> A remark to make:—I am grateful to you for proving indubitably that if Landor had been a contemporary, he'd have been as determined a Jingo as Louis, as I, or as A. C. S. [Swinburne] himself.[1]

Colvin ignored the taunt in the belief that his friend's jingoism was not to be taken seriously. But when he heard that both Henley and Stevenson were planning contributions to Alfred Austin's *National Review*, he lost all patience with the would-be Conservatives; Henley was a "Beaconsfieldian by a literary whim," and Louis was merely "the son of his father"; neither had ever "thought about politics at all." As for Austin, he seemed to Colvin simply a "little whipper-snapping all-round failure, . . the best kind of an editor they could get."[2] Nevertheless, if Stevenson had unthinkingly accepted his father's political sympathies and made them his own, he proved himself, at least in this one respect, an unusually dutiful son. His Conservatism was fired to white heat by the news of Gordon's death at Khartoum; and to the "Grand Old Man" whom he held responsible for the tragedy, he drafted a letter subscribed "Your fellow-criminal in the sight of God."[3] His hatred of Gladstone colored even his literary judgments[4]; he was chagrined beyond words by the fact that the French edition of *Treasure Island* had sold well partly on the recommendation of the British Prime Minister.[5] Like-

[1] Quoted by Lucas, *The Colvins*, p. 139.
[2] See Lucas, pp. 157-58.
[3] See Will Low, *Chronicle of Friendships*, p. 333.
[4] Contrast Henley's distinction between politics and criticism; see below, p. 142.
[5] See Low, p. 332.

wise, Henley, whether or not he had ever "thought about politics at all," adopted an attitude of unmitigated scorn for Liberalism and of unswerving allegiance to its antithesis. While he would concede the imbecility of Alfred Austin, he saw nothing "foolish" or futile in his plans for a Tory review. He refused to "drop" or to conceal his determined jingoism. On interviewing William Archer for the first time in the office of the *Magazine of Art*, he found occasion to enquire:

> "By the way—one thing more. What are your politics?"
> "Well!" [Archer] replied, taken aback, . . "that is a rather large order."
> "In one word," he said, . . "are you a Conservative?"
> "In one word," [Archer] replied, . . "no!"
> "Oh!" was his sole comment; and though the vowel rhymed to the ear, it expressed to the mind a sharp and untunable dissonance.[6]

Thus in the mid 'eighties, Henley's political prejudice was, like his style, "an open secret." Nevertheless, art, not politics, was his major concern. While his interest in Constable or Dumas, Rodin or Dickens, Mozart or Rembrandt flagged not nor failed, he frequently grew weary of the phlegmatic Salisbury and the inscrutable Gladstone and all their endless petty bickerings about Home Rule and socialism and foreign policy. In such moods he welcomed escape into "the sunny-eyed heroic age" of Homer, when all was "energy and tact and valour and resource, as [became] the captain of an indomitable human soul," when "men were not afraid of life nor ashamed of death, and you could be heroic without a dread of clever editors."[7] But as the decade progressed he found escape increasingly impossible. Retired from the *Magazine of Art*, he was no longer inhibited by the standards of his employers; he was free to express in his brilliant talk his highly personal opin-

[6] Quoted by Charles Archer, *William Archer*, pp. 120-21.
[7] *Works*, IV, 84, 86-87.

ions. Yet in his freedom he felt a new constraint; he was called upon to clarify his own relationship to the society in which he moved. Yeats, who had imagined him to be "without political interests or convictions," soon found him growing "into a violent unionist and imperialist."[8] From Yeats's point of view this was a lamentable metamorphosis. From Henley's it was a necessary recognition that the unconquerable soul had significance only in a social context. Whereas the art journal had been of its essence a more or less "aesthetic" publication, the *Scots Observer* was designed as a larger criticism of life. Not only was it to treat of books and paintings; it was also to take a definite stand on the political issues of the day. And its subtitle, "An Imperial Review," would make clear its political bias.

Colvin's charge that Henley was a "Beaconsfieldian by a literary whim" was not entirely unfounded. By the 'seventies the Victorian political complex had resolved itself into one tremendous duel between Gladstone and Disraeli; and there could be little doubt as to which of these would win the respect of an invalid whose knowledge of literature was of necessity far deeper and broader than his experience with life. To Henley Gladstone seemed a humorless classicist, a Comtian with a dogged religious faith, a friend of John Morley's with a persistent belief in political compromise. Disraeli, on the other hand, appeared as the glittering novelist who had combined the passion of Byron with the wit and wisdom of Voltaire; he was "the Uncommonplace incarnate, the antithesis of Grocerdom," "assuredly the most romantic . . . figure of his time." In him the student of style found a beneficent influence, "a great artist in life renowned for memorable speech," whereas in Gladstone he could find only "a man of many words and no sayings":

He is the prince of agitators, but it would be impossible for him to mint a definition of "agitation"; he is

8 William Butler Yeats, *Autobiography* (New York, 1938), p. 109.

the world's most eloquent arithmetician, but it is beyond him to epigrammatise the fact that two and two make four.[9]

Still, Gladstone's was probably the stronger "temperament," the more immediate personality. For Disraeli never descended to the level of his public; he stood forever aloof, in ironic detachment, above his world: "He was as incapable of such a feat as Mr. Gladstone's Midlothian campaign as Mr. Gladstone is of producing the gaming scene in *The Young Duke.*" But the very fact that Disraeli remained "to the general . . . a kind of caviare," a thing to be valued rather than trusted—this alone recommended him to a youth who was himself in aesthetic and intellectual revolt against the gods of acceptance. Beaconsfield bearing "peace with honour" from the war-mongers of Berlin, commandeering adulation from the factions that once had despised him, was as much Disraeli's work of art as the less confident Endymion unsealing the letter that called him to the premiership. His life-story was cast in dramatic mould with the result that it could be read only in dramatic terms. Insofar then as the character might so be interpreted, Henley was a Beaconsfieldian by a literary whim, or more accurately, by a well-considered literary judgment.

By 1881 Disraeli was dead; and Gladstone, already well past his prime, had entered upon his second ministry, alone, estranged from his own talented cabinet, without a Tory rival sufficiently strong to awaken the fullness of his power. The conflict had lost its personal extension; the drama was gone. And what had been a literary prejudice became a matter of political principle. In his antipathy to Gladstone, Henley was driven naturally to identify the long vision of Disraeli with the comparatively short-sighted Conservative opposition. And eventually the extremes of Liberal isolationism led the most lethargic of Tories to a national and imperial policy

[9] *Works*, IV, 22.

far beyond Disraeli's wildest imagining. No longer primarily a clash between two gifted leaders, the warfare between the parties emphasized the essentials of each contending ideology. Accordingly, when Henley assumed control of the *Scots Observer*, he felt assured of the definite strength of the Tory idealism and the distinct rightness of the Tory cause. On the first anniversary of the paper, he printed a statement of his editorial standards, which might serve to indicate the nature of his loyalties; the *Scots Observer*, he said, had not once been false to any of its ideals, but had "had its say, and with no uncertain sound," on "the vital—the imperial quality of politics, the characteristics of the Scottish nation, the relation of that nation to the great Empire of which that nation forms a part." Four years later, in answer to a complaint that the Conservative press lacked popular appeal, he reasserted his demand for a high-principled anti-demagogic political theory:

> Toryism, as I conceive it, is as much a matter of taste as a body of doctrine, and as much a mental attitude as a set of principles. . . . Toryism, to be plain, is in some sort a matter of aversions—one aversion is for that conspiracy of bad public breeding and individual prurience which "one may term popular culture."[10]

Such were his idealism and his taste; and his subsequent failure as a political journalist arose largely from his refusal to sacrifice that idealism and that taste to the interests of a middle-class reading public.

At no time did Henley think of the Tory party as the reactionary group in English politics. Paradoxical as it may seem, he equated Conservatism with Radicalism; in his memoir of George Steevens, he remarked that his protégé had never wavered in imperial fervor—

> he was too good an Englishman and too poor a hypocrite. That, despite his Toryism, he remained a philosophical Radical is like enough. I have yet to learn, in

[10] *National Review*, xxi (1893), 268-71.

131

fact, that there is any very considerable difference between the several points of view.[11]

But the paradox is more apparent than real. For the Toryism to which Henley subscribed was a broad doctrine of individual freedom within the fabric of a firm but self-reformative social structure. Yet for the practical, the "unphilosophical," Radical who would have had freedom without discipline, on the one hand, or authority without liberty, on the other, he had no tolerance. The one of these alternatives, the anarchy of complete, self-seeking individualism, was by the 'eighties a decreasing menace; while the other, the tyranny of suppressed individualism, seemed an imminent danger, and a danger which the government did nothing effectively to counter. While successive parliaments pursued indeterminate foreign policies, Henley saw Socialism gaining strength at home. And it was Socialism that threatened to impose upon him the will of a Philistine mob and so to destroy his independence as thinker and artist. The *Scots Observer*, therefore, insisted upon the long-established values of individual enterprise:

> Supposing we went only as far as the Germans have gone towards a complete system of State Socialism, we should be as the Germans—all educated and dull alike; we should march and work in well-drilled gangs; we should be subdued by a severe uniformity and invaded by a dreary pessimism; we should lose that enthusiasm of original effort which is the very salt of our life; and we should lose completely all proper understanding of literature and art.[12]

As an antidote to Hyndman and the Fabians and the misguided aspiration of the rising Laborites, there remained the example of Disraeli in whose controlled democracy lay England's "one defence against socialism and the dominion of the Common Fool." The theory of

[11] Henley, "Memoir," G. W. Steevens, *Things Seen* (Edinburgh, 1900), p. xvii, n.
[12] "Socialism in Excelsis," *Scots Observer*, i (1889), 377.

political individualism could alone satisfy the activist's demand for an unhampered exercise of his own free will.[13]

Despite its well-defined hatreds, Toryism was not merely "a matter of aversions"; nor were Henley's political writings wholly destructive. His every attack on Gladstone's "little Englandism" implied his positive faith in the ideal of a unified, though far-flung, British Empire. And in his imperialism, which ran counter to the official Liberal policy, he found considerable "Radical" support. The more progressive members of Gladstone's own cabinet, Lord Rosebery, Joseph Chamberlain, Sir Charles Dilke, demanded of their leader a fuller recognition of Britain's colonial obligations. Rosebery in his fourteen months as Prime Minister proved himself an imperialist as ardent as Kipling. Chamberlain, who had opposed Home Rule,[14] finally seceded to the Tory camp, whence he was to lead England vigorously through the·African war. A lesser statesman than either of these, Dilke made an early and significant contribution to the late Victorian imperialist movement; in 1868 he published *Greater Britain*, a travel book designed to show the true extent of British power:

> The idea which in all the length of my travels has been at once my fellow and my guide—a key wherewith to unlock the hidden things of strange new lands—is a conception, however imperfect, of the grandeur of our race, already girdling the world, which it is destined, perhaps, eventually to overspread. . . .

Even the Socialist could appreciate the imperial impulse; Hyndman believed that "the Anglo-Saxon race, which [had] shown the world how to reconcile freedom and order with steady progress, [could] by combination

[13] *Cf.* Stevenson's attack on Socialism, "The Day after Tomorrow," *Contemporary Review*, LI (1887), 472-79.

[14] Henley's paper had defended Chamberlain's stand before his final break with the Liberals; see "A Unionist Radical," *Scots Observer*, I (1889), 321-22.

and determined effort secure for themselves and their children leadership in the social changes which [were] close at hand."[15] Such diverse concern with Britain's imperial mission indicates the wide appeal of an essentially Tory doctrine. For the Tories alone as a party, from the time of Disraeli's Crystal Palace address, remained consistently faithful to the imperial policy. Hyndman exerted scant influence over the workers to whom he had dedicated his capital; and Dilke, Rosebery, and Chamberlain were from the first dissentient elements in the Liberal ranks.

It may be that the rise of imperialism was coincident with the decline of interest in theological disputation.[16] Certainly by the last decade of the century, the concept of a national or racial absolute inspired a fervor comparable to that engendered by the older evangelical religion; a fanatic faith in the collective destiny of the English peoples absorbed much of the emotional energy that had been poured into mid-Victorian Protestantism. Still the myth of the Saxon race was by no means a *fin-de-siècle* invention; years before Henley or Kipling, Charles Kingsley had sung of English blood and English conquest:

> What's the soft South-wester?
> 'Tis the ladies' breeze,
> Bringing home their turtle-loves
> Out of all the seas:
> But the black North-easter,
> Through the snowstorm hurled,
> Drives our English hearts of oak
> Seaward round the world.
> Come, as came your fathers,
> Heralded by thee,
> Conquering from the eastward,
> Lords by land and sea.

[15] H. M. Hyndman, *England for All* (London, 1881), p. 168.
[16] See G. K. Chesterton, *Autobiography* (New York, 1936), pp. 144-45; and *cf.* James Raymond Sontag, *Germany and England: Background of Conflict* (New York, 1938), p. 115.

134

Come; and strong within us
Stir the Vikings' blood;
Bracing brain and sinew;
Blow, thou wind of God.

But there was this difference between Kingsley's Englandism and the later imperialism: to the Christian Socialist, England and the Anglican Church were inter-
dependent entities, and it was the Englishman's spiritual
duty to carry Anglican truth even unto the ends of the
earth; to the Tory idealist England was a civilized, if
agnostic, democracy, and it was the white man's burden
to ensure the preservation of his country and his race
against the inroads of barbarism.

Early in the year 1890 the *Barrack Room Ballads* of
Rudyard Kipling arrived in manuscript at the office of
the *Scots Observer*. Overjoyed at his good fortune, Henley straightway declaimed the song of Danny Deever
to his admiring staff. Though such rollicking ditties contributed to the unpopularity, and so to the eventual
failure, of the paper that dared print them, they made
of Kipling the uncrowned laureate of Greater Britain.[17]
Henley's own imperialist verse lacked the dramatic appeal of the *Ballads*, but attained through subjective
lyricism a greater personal intensity. Whereas Kipling
admired the Motherland by reasoned conviction, Henley loved it from instinctive emotion, irrationally and
for its own sake.[18] A deep-seated faith in the infallibility
of England, a desire to serve and to sacrifice, lay behind
his "*Pro Rege Nostro*," surely one of the great patriotic
lyrics in the language:

Ever the faith endures,
England, my England:—

[17] The *Ballads* were apparently not well received till their appearance in book-form in 1892. *Cf.* Henley's testimony: "I do not think
they did the journal any good, these songs of the barrack and the
march: fresh, vigorous, *vécues*, surpassingly suggestive as they were.
. . . In fact I know they did it none at all."—"Concerning Atkins,"
Pall Mall Magazine, xxi (1900), 283.

[18] *Cf.* Chesterton, *Heretics* (London, 1938), p. 40.

135

"Take and break us: we are yours,
    England, my own!
Life is good, and joy runs high
Between English earth and sky:
Death is death; but we shall die
    To the Song on your bugles blown, England—
    To the stars on your bugles blown!"

Lines like these epitomize the best in a Tory tradition: the faith in a national ideal reaching "down the years," the responsibility for a master-work in cultural achievement, the sheer joy in the green earth of Shakespeare's "scepter'd isle" and those "dear demi-Englands, far-away isles of home." Yet the poem has no palpable design upon the reader; it is not intended to propagate the politics of imperialism. It represents simply and sincerely the poet's devotion to his country and his "race."

In view of latter-day racial heresies, it is perhaps pertinent to examine the implications of Henley's "faith in blood and star." Nowhere in his prose or verse may be found the slightest evidence of anti-Semitism, from the taint of which later British Tories have not been entirely free. Nowhere in his criticism is there a refusal to understand and to accept the conventions of foreign art; on the contrary, there is frequently a tendency to repudiate English craftsmanship, in order to commend a more exotic creative talent. If Henley's pride in race means anything at all, it can be interpreted only as a belief in the *genius loci* of England, a belief that the very air of Britain breathed a tradition of individual freedom and democratic law. Given variant circumstances, this belief approximates Walt Whitman's conception of an American race destined to emerge from the placement of a liberated protestant spirit in an almost infinite geographical vastitude. However tenuous or incapable of intellectual proof such creeds may be, they have a moral and emotional soundness far beyond the absurd perversions of a hypothetical Aryanism. And they have this validity: that in the long run a nation or a culture lives by faith in its own heritage and in the positive ideals that have insured its existence.

One aspect of Henley's Englandism seems incomprehensible not only intellectually but also in the light of normal emotional experience. This doctrine is compressed into one line of the *"Pro Rege Nostro"*; England is, among other things, "Spouse-in-Chief of the ancient Sword." Insofar as the Sword was aboriginally the prerequisite factor in the nation's survival, the Sword became, by Henleyan logic, the symbol of all cultural advance, and consequently, a good in itself. Present throughout his war poems, this idea is developed most fully in *The Song of the Sword*, published in 1892 and dedicated to Rudyard Kipling. Anglo-Saxon "kennings" serve to define the Sword as

> The War-Thing, the Comrade,
> Father of honour
> And giver of kingship,
> The fame-smith, the song-master. . . .
> Ho! then, the sound
> Of my voice, the implacable
> Angel of Destiny!—
> I am the Sword.

So conceived, the Sword becomes chief agent of the creative Will in shaping reality:

> Thrust through the fatuous,
> Thrust through the fungous brood,
> Spawned in my shadow
> And gross with my gift! . . .
> Follow, O, follow me
> Till the waste places
> All the gray globe over
> Ooze, as the honeycomb
> Drips, with the sweetness
> Distilled of my strength.

Obviously the sanction behind this mystical belligerency is a naïve and misapplied Darwinism. The Sword is the nisus of the evolutionary process, the great natural selector, the Will of God:

> Sifting the nations,
> The slag from the metal,
> The waste and the weak
> From the fit and the strong;
> Fighting the brute,
> The abysmal Fecundity; . . .
> Clear singing, clean slicing;
> Sweet spoken, soft finishing;
> Making death beautiful. . . .
> Arch-anarch, chief builder,
> Prince and evangelist,
> I am the Will of God:
> I am the Sword.

"Sifting the nations" with the mental detachment of the scientist, "making death beautiful" with the dispassionate skill of the surgeon—so the invalid thwarted in his longing for physical action dreamed of battle. Theoretically war had meaning; it gave the opportunity of heroism to a sedentary, materialistic world. Death for an ideal seemed preferable to the life of purposeless passivity:

> . . . To drowse with the fen behind and the fog before,
> When rain-rot spreads, and a tame sea mumbles the
> shore,
> Not to adventure, none to fight, no right and no wrong,
> Sons of the Sword heart-sick for a stave of your sire's
> old song—
> O, you envy the blessèd dead that can live no more!

Pathological in character, this war-and-death philosophy was but another expression of the masculine protest against preordained weakness. But even in Henley's case, the delight in blood and battle was programmatic and doctrinaire in its development, tried by a merely vicarious experience. Consequently, under the stress of actual warfare it suffered serious modification. The conflict in South Africa altered the whole concept of militarism.

To the astute Colonial Secretary, Joseph Chamberlain, the Boer War involved distinct economic issues on which Britain's imperial well-being depended. To Henley the war was from the outset a matter of principle, a severe test of British morale. Looking back over the nineteenth century, he could see a time-honored idealism gradually smothered by an ascendant materialism:

> We wanted to make money; and we made it. We began to minimise our importance in the comity of peoples; to misread the results of our tremendous experience; to argue that our fathers had been common fools, and that our destiny was quite other than they believed.[19]

But the African war would change all this; if Britain was to be victorious, Britons must find a new value in national tradition, a new faith in their heritage. Accordingly, in the first of his lyrics *For England's Sake* after the outbreak of hostilities, he remonstrated with his countrymen:

> Where is our ancient pride of heart?
> Our faith in blood and star?
> Who would but marvel how we came
> If this were all we are?

Then, with the rallying of imperial forces from north, south, east, and west, his jingoism reached a mad intensity. In high excitement he wrote doggerel songs to old music-hall tunes:

> From Gib to Vancouver, from Thames to Yukon,
> The live air is loud with you—*Storm along, John!*

> Let but the bugles of England play
> *Over the hills and far away!*

But as the imperial crusade sank into the long, exhausting siege, his enthusiasm shifted to a fearful hysteria. With bitter satisfaction he heard of Lord Roberts's hard-won successes against regiments of the treacherous enemy:

[19] *PMM*, xxi, 281.

By the dismal fords, the thankless hills, the desolate,
　half-dead flats
He has shepherded them like silly sheep, and cornered
　them like rats.

He has driven and headed them strength by strength,
　as a hunter deals with his deer,
And has filled the place of the heart in their breast with
　a living devil of fear.

The snarling violence of these miserable rhymes stands
in marked contrast to the religious fervor of the *"Pro
Rege Nostro."* In theory war had meant "the glory of
battle and adventure." In practice it proved a grim
tragedy of "toil for the race, and pain, and peril, and
death." And death itself no longer seemed the sweet
fruition of an earthly struggle. Of the slaughter of British
youth in South Africa, he found "it impossible to speak
soberly."[20] Their "passing for England's sake . . . thrilled
the ends of the world with pain and pride," not because
they went forth careless of life, but because they acted
in accordance with an inner call to duty, a conviction
that England's righteous ideals lay in jeopardy; "many
hundreds of brave and brilliant and beautiful creatures,
. . at the especial instance of the mad and criminal old
man at Pretoria," had chosen to die rather than to suffer
"an insolent and monstrous wrong" to the cause of Empire.[21] But the true tragedy of war lay less in the presence of casualty lists than in the appalling fact that a
national crisis shaking the very roots of a civilization
could alone procure a national unity, that human beings
would co-operate only under an inhuman compulsion.
Towards the end of the conflict Henley made his eloquent and dreadful commentary on the state of democratic society. Peace, "the White Angel," returning to a
land, "storm-wrought, a place of quakes, all thunder-
scarred," restores prosperity and "a large, full-stom-
ached faith in kindliness," until once again

[20] *PMM*, xxi, 135.　　　　　　[21] "Memoir," *Things Seen*, p. ix.

the nation, in a dream
Of money and love and sport, hangs at the paps
Of well-being, and so
Goes fattening, mellowing, dozing, rotting down
Into a rich deliquium of decay.

Only War, "the Red Angel, the Awakener," can recall a
culture from its spiritual decadence; in ruin and grief,

A people, haggard with defeat,
Asks if there be a God; yet sets its teeth,
Faces calamity, and goes into the fire
Another than it was . . .
New-pithed, new-souled, new-visioned.

As grim "Epilogue" to the verses *For England's Sake*,
this poem represents the invalid's final attempt to find
a pattern of meaning in the chaos of conflict and so to
reconcile an illogical lust for battle with a deep sorrow
for the "brave and beautiful" war-dead. Henley survived the Peace of Vereeniging by less than fourteen
months. But in that time he saw the validity of his own
prediction. The White Angel came bearing "a full-stom-
ached faith in kindliness"; and benevolent Englishmen,
free to quarrel among themselves, began to question
the wisdom of their war-policy. Chamberlain returned
from South Africa in March, 1903, to a land of little
Englanders hostile to his plans for colonial preference.
The ardor of the Tory Jingos was spent; and the nation
as a whole, weary of imperial problems, prepared to
welcome the reforms of a resurgent Liberal party.

The product of a general war-hysteria and a personal
sense of weakness, Henley's brutal songs *For England's
Sake* were, in the last analysis, nothing more than spo-
radic effusions. Never was Henley guilty of the sustained
bathos that transforms Doughty's *Cliffs* into a ludicrous,
if unconscious, burlesque of the imperialist sentiment.
Despite his most inordinate bombast, he could never
long mistake the martial scene for the whole stage of
human experience. His elegy to the Empress-Queen,

141

written at the peak of the war, lists the exploits of English soldiery as but one element in the great Victorian composite:

> Think of the mighty ghosts: soldiers and priests,
> Artists and captains of discovery,
> God's chosen, His adventurers up the heights
> Of thought and deed—how many of them that led
> The forlorn hopes of the World!—
> Her peers and servants, made the air
> Of her death-chamber glorious! Think how they thronged
> About her bed, and with what pride
> They took this sister-ghost
> Tenderly into the night!

Of his sympathy with the artists, the creators, the captains of discovery, Henley made a life-work; in his Tory imperialism, he found an earnest, but entirely subordinate, avocation. "The Tory party, without a qualm, let die alike the *National Observer* and the *New Review*," not because it was, as Mr. Ford Madox Ford alleges,[22] "the stupid party," but because it could find other and more popular organs of propaganda. For Henley was, throughout his career as journalist, much more deeply concerned with his own editorial standards than with the promotion of any political ideology. And the Tory prejudice, however essential and sincere, had surprisingly small effect on his literary judgments. An ardent royalist, he could forget far more readily than Dr. Johnson that Milton had been "a surly and acrimonious republican." And his distaste for Gladstone was not so great that he would refuse one of the aged statesman's last essays on literature, submitted for publication in his *New Review*.[23] "The interest of art," he said, "is absolutely incompatible with the sentiment of patriotism,"[24] and therefore also with the dictates of the

[22] Ford Madox Hueffer (Ford), *Memories and Impressions* (New York, 1911), p. 193.

[23] See "Man-Making and Verse-Making," *New Review*, xv (1896), 116-28.

[24] *Works*, iv, 333.

authoritarian state; art demanded freedom of spirit, the right to function in its own way apart from all political considerations. The era of Napoleon was aesthetically dead, because "the despot in him had precedence of the artist; and as a despot he had no love for new ideas and no tolerance for intellectual independence. . . . He could turn out generals and administrators by the dozen; but it was a different matter when he came to deal with art and artists."[25] The liberty to form and express political opinion, conservative or radical, had for Henley its deepest meaning in that it implied the coextensive liberty to exercise an individual creative talent.

By the Liberals Henley was regarded less as a dangerous political enemy than as a distinguished man of letters.[26] And to the Tories his imperialism seemed less significant than his influence as literary critic and lyric poet. A. J. Balfour granted him a civil-list pension for his services to literature, a year before the African war and the writing of the uneven verses *For England's Sake*. And George Wyndham, the most promising young Conservative since Balfour, joined his circle not to learn politics, but to study the principles of English prose composition. It was Henley who told him, "You will not make the worse Prime Minister or even Irish Secretary for having done a good piece of critical literature. A style is worth having, at whatever cost."[27] And it was with Henley's advice and encouragement that he brought forth his admirable editions of Shakespeare's *Poems* and of North's *Plutarch*.

While Henley's Tory bias had a very real place in the development of his own social philosophy, his best work in prose and verse was free from party doctrine; and

[25] *Works*, IV, 226-27.
[26] Yeats, Madox Ford, and Arthur Waugh all disagreed with his politics, but admired his critical abilities. Masterman, Liberal whip in the Asquith government, loathed Henley's political entourage, but valued his poetry; see below, p. 155.
[27] Quoted by J. W. Mackail and Guy Wyndham, *The Life and Letters of George Wyndham*, 2 vols. (London, n.d.), I, 53.

his love of things English bore little relation to the political and economic problems of his time. Far beyond working-class unrest and parliamentary debate stretched the British tradition of "beef, beer, horses, *Moll Flanders* and the Church of England, the King and *The Newgate Calendar*,—what is there, what could there be more typically English than all these?"[28] These were tangible realities; and in these Henley believed not with the intellectual conviction of the reasonable Tory, but with the emotional instinct of the lyric poet. "England, my England!"—this was his heritage; and his love of this ideal alone among his political dogmas had considerable place in his literary criticism. Whereas in his apprenticeship he had declared the value of French art, in his maturity he turned towards the English eighteenth century. And when all his political prejudice is forgotten, it remains his permanent achievement that through his enthusiasm for the Augustan ages he led a whole generation of English writers away from a sterile romantic decadence back to the humor and the realism of their lustier forebears.

[28] *Works*, II, 400.

PART IV. THE AUTOCRAT OF TASTE

PAINTER: It is a pretty mocking of the life.
Here is a touch; is't good?

POET: I will say of it,
It tutors nature: artificial strife
Lives in these touches, livelier than life.

—TIMON OF ATHENS, Act I, Sc. 1.

LATE in the spring of 1890 Oscar Wilde's first extended prose-work, *The Picture of Dorian Gray,* appeared in *Lippincott's Magazine.* As an aesthetic achievement, the tale was, in Wilde's own opinion, so "perfect," so "complete," that only an amoral Goethe or a Gautier could fully have appreciated it; and one might hope "that some ghostly publisher [was] even now distributing shadowy copies in the Elysian fields, and that the cover of Gautier's copy [was] covered with gilt asphodels."[1] Week after week throughout the summer, the author's appreciations of his masterpiece and the divergent opinions of readers and critics were printed in the correspondence section of Henley's *Scots Observer,* under the title, "Art and Morality." Outparadoxed by Charles Whibley's contention that *Dorian Gray* contained "lots of morality and no art," Wilde eventually resigned from the debate, professing, in a letter filling two columns of small type, heartily to "dislike newspaper controversies of any kind." Though Henley remained ironically aloof from the quarrel,[2] he drew satisfaction from the belief that several of the correspondents had chosen his own *Views and Reviews* as a touchstone of judgment. Issued in the same month as Wilde's novel, this little volume, "a mosaic of scraps and shreds recovered from the shot rubbish of some fourteen years of journalism," crystallized Henley's literary reputation. When the poet-critic descended upon London early in November to attend the *première* of *Beau Austin,* he found himself generally esteemed as a brilliant and versatile man of letters. Before the New Year he had transferred his periodical from Thistle Street to the Strand and had rechristened it the

---

[1] Oscar Wilde, *Scots Observer,* IV (1890), 332.
[2] Wilde accused Henley of writing the letters signed "H." But "H.," who stood for all the ideals and prejudices of the typical Philistine, denied that his name was Henley. See *SO,* IV, 333, 384.

National Observer. There on Wilde's own ground, he firmly established himself, a formidable rival for the literary dictatorship of the 'nineties.

Henley returned to England at the height of his powers, assured of his critical position, prepared vigorously to counter the movement towards "decadence." Nor was he alone in his campaign as "realist." Two years in Edinburgh had given him opportunity to indoctrinate with his principles a whole band of young writers, each of whom admired his penetration and worshiped his energy. To them Henley had proven that the aesthetes were aesthetically, as well as intellectually, effete, and that Nature was now and always man's gallant protest against Art. In their bright lexicon there was no such word as "quail"; all was stoic defiance and savage onslaught; "pretence of any kind was the red rag; 'bleat' was the unpardonable sin; the man who was 'human' was the man to be praised."[3] Henley was assuredly human—"human," said Yeats, "like one of Shakespeare's characters—and yet pressed and pummelled, as it were, into a single attitude, almost into a gesture and a speech as by some overwhelming situation."[4] His "masculine protest" against weakness, delicacy, aestheticism, itself had become stylized. If in his verse he wrote an intense spiritual autobiography, exposing his frailty and his fear and in turn clothing both in a bravado of fine phrases, in his commerce with the world he betrayed only an unwavering faith in the value of courageous living and the strength and purpose of his own individuality. He strove consciously to preserve the illusion of hearty self-assurance and unbroken self-confidence. He was content to have himself looked upon as the bold buccaneer who had plundered the treasure house of literature and spoke whereof he knew. His true triumph over chance and circumstance lay in his knowledge that to "the intellectual flower of young England" he ap-

[3] Elizabeth Robins Pennell, *Nights* (London, 1916), p. 136.
[4] Yeats, *Autobiography*, p. 109.

W. E. HENLEY (1892)
By Leslie Ward ("Spy")

peared "the Viking chief of letters, whom all delighted to follow, whose praise alone mattered, whose example set the mark for rejoicing emulation."[5] The affinity to John Silver had grown closer with the passing of the years; and whereas he once had resented Stevenson's caricature, he now cherished the resemblance. Mrs. Pennell tells us that William Nicholson in painting him was so "preoccupied with the big soft hat and blue shirt and flowing tie" that he "turned him into a brigand, a land pirate," to the great joy of Henley, whom she "always suspected of feeling this value himself and dressing as he did for the sake of picturesqueness."[6] Yet the piratic pose, if it might be called a "pose," was maintained so consistently that none but the most discerning critic could recognize its affectation. At times even Yeats felt the artifice so like nature as to be the man's "true self." Few others doubted for a moment his absolute sincerity. Gilbert Parker saw in him one who had struggled valiantly with life and had concluded that the world was "a good battleground where you [might] fight and bury your dead in a fine gentlemanly manner."[7] And Leslie Cornford found him "a strong and lusty man among men who had rubbed shoulders with the world, and had looked undismayed upon the worst of it, . . rooted in the good earth like an oak, whose branches took the wind and the sunshine, and pointed to the stars."[8] Somewhat diffident about his own work, Conrad approached the Viking chief cautiously; and on winning from him due approval, he wrote bravely to Edward Garnett, "Now I have conquered Henley, I aint fraid of the divvle himself."[9] Aubrey Beardsley's experience was less fortunate; on his arrival, portfolio in hand, at the offices of the *National Observer*, he had been so

[5] Francis Thompson, *Current Literature*, xxxv (1903), 364.

[6] Pennell, *Nights*, p. 127.

[7] Gilbert Parker, *Lippincott's Magazine*, lii (1893), 114.

[8] Cornford, *Henley*, p. 97.

[9] Quoted by Elizabeth Robins Pennell, *The Life and Letters of Joseph Pennell*, 2 vols. (Boston, 1929), i, 247.

149

terrified by the editor's ferocious aspect that he fled posthaste down the stairs, clutching his drawings to his bosom.[10] Such anecdotes indicate how large loomed the figure of Henley at a time when colorful personality far outweighed creative production. Oscar Wilde's arrogance could hardly have seemed more compelling.

Nevertheless, Henley's fierce demeanor would not alone have insured his personal dominance of a sophisticated literary society. If his ringing voice attracted passing attention, his powers of speech commanded lasting respect. By all reports, he was "one of the great talkers of his time,"[11] a warm enthusiast, a master of invective, a man of humor and passion. Max Beerbohm declared that there was "more joy in [his] breast over one oath roared by Mr. Henley than over the ninety-and-nine just opinions which a man like Mr. Archer could produce at a moment's notice."[12] But a talent for blasphemy was less than half of Henley's endowment as conversation-maker. Anathematizing or eulogizing, he never spoke at random; always he had the knack of adapting his tone to the subject under discussion and to the taste or distaste of his auditors. At the Savile Club he chatted quietly with Thomas Hardy. At the Berkeley Hotel in Sussex he teasingly decried Mallarmé to one of Mallarmé's most determined admirers.[13] Under Kensington clock he disagreed politely for over an hour with George Saintsbury as to whether or not Thackeray were really a gentleman after all.[14] If the occasion demanded he could exercise a roguish irony. Savagely he ruffled the composure of Henry James whom he charged with inexcusable neglect of Mrs. Oliphant's *Kirsteen*. Cowed

[10] See Pennell, *Nights*, p. 139.

[11] E. V. Lucas, *Reading, Writing, and Remembering* (London, 1932), p. 170. *Cf.* Pennell, *Nights*, pp. 132-37.

[12] Max Beerbohm, *Around Theatres*, 2 vols. (New York, 1930), I, 56.

[13] See Paul Leroi, "William-Ernest Henley," *L'Art*, LXII (1903), 410.

[14] See J. W. Cunliffe, *Leaders of the Victorian Revolution* (New York, 1934), pp. 95-96.

into submission, James hastened to peruse the commended novel, only to find that "the poor woman" who
wrote it "had a simply feminine conception of literature."[15] Wilde, who lacked James's high seriousness, was
less likely to be silenced by an ironical rebuff. Yet he
found it almost impossible to confute a Henleyan dictum; Henley, he said at the end of his life, was the only
man who ever had taxed to the full his intellect and ingenuity.[16] This was high praise indeed to come from the
artist in epigram. And Henley after Wilde's death returned the compliment; Wilde was clever, he told Will
Low—"Clever? I should say he was. Seated where you
are he has held the table against *me*, more than once."[17]
Each envying the other his skill in dialectic, Wilde and
Henley clashed repeatedly in hot argument. Finally the
"realist's" was the victory of force; disgusted beyond
measure by a persistent mental perversity, he eventually
propelled the "decadent" with angry crutch down the
steps of a Soho café.[18] But Wilde's was the Parthian
shaft; commenting on Henley's vigor of expression, he
wrote: "His personality is insistent. To converse with
him is a physical no less than an intellectual recreation."[19]

Not all the aesthetes, however, were to be convinced
by flashing repartee or felled by flying crutch. Careless
of Henley's opinions, the Rhymers' Club met weekly at
the Cheshire Cheese to decide the fate of minor verse.
And it was through the dubious repute of these *fin-de-
siècle* romantics that the last decade of Victoria's reign
passed into literary history as the "yellow" 'nineties.
Nevertheless, though the Henleyan activists enjoyed
less notoriety, theirs was, as we shall see, the far more

[15] See E. F. Benson, *Final Edition* (New York, 1940), p. 10.
[16] See Vincent O'Sullivan, *Aspects of Wilde* (London, 1936), p. 96.
Cf. Alfred Douglas, *Autobiography* (London, 1929), p. 78.
[17] See Low, *A Chronicle of Friendships*, p. 475.
[18] See J. M. Barrie, *The Greenwood Hat* (London, 1937), p. 195.
[19] Quoted by William Rothenstein, *Men and Memories*, 2 vols.
(New York, 1931), I, 312.

enduring influence in modern English letters. Long after each of the Rhymers had died,[20] like Enoch Soames, of his own decadence, the realists remained, a link between the old art and the new. Even before the decline of the aesthetic school, the men of the *National Observer* had organized a rival coterie. Rallying 'round their intrepid editor, and so constituting what Beerbohm facetiously called "the Henley Regatta,"[21] they assembled at Solferino's Restaurant in Rupert Street, there to "regulate all literature till all hours of the morning."[22] Charles Whibley, Rudyard Kipling, George Wyndham, George Steevens, Wilfred Pollock, Gilbert Parker, Vernon Blackburn, Leslie Cornford, W. B. Yeats, G. S. Street, H. B. Marriott-Watson—some of these would pass into oblivion with the periodical for which they wrote; but some would outwear the greatest of the "decadents." Yet however each might subsequently fare, each made his own contribution to the golden talk at Solferino's; and each paid willing tribute to his crippled chieftain with the wonderful gift of tongues. To Sidney Low "it was like a glimpse into the old Bohemia that has passed away, to see Henley lounging at the head of the table with his bodyguard ranged round a very festal board, while quip, and crook, and shrewd criticism, and Rabelaisian jest were bandied from hand to hand, under a floating cloud of tobacco-smoke."[23] "Henley," said Yeats, "got the best out of us all, because he had made us accept him as our judge and we knew that his judgment could neither sleep, nor be softened, nor changed, nor turned aside."[24] For all his surface mannerism, the poseur was essentially a man of deep conviction and genuine intellectual vitality. It was not remarkable that

[20] I do not forget Ernest Rhys and Arthur Symons; but these were always something more, and less, than Rhymers.

[21] See Rothenstein, I, 285.

[22] Rudyard Kipling, *Something of Myself* (London, 1934), p. 82.

[23] Sidney Low, *Living Age*, CCXXXIX (1903), 155.

[24] Yeats, p. 112.

the Regatta adopted his idiom, his prejudices, even his gestures.

On Thursday evenings after the *National Observer* had gone to press, the more ardent of the disciples would follow the master en masse to the home of Joseph Pennell in Buckingham Street. There, over whiskeys-and-soda, the host and his guests would review the sorry state of art and society. Long afterwards Mrs. Pennell recalled Henley's loud voice and contagious laugh: "Never, anywhere else have I heard such talk. . . . In my memory, every Thursday night stands for a battle. Henley was then always at his best."[25]

Throughout the early 'nineties, at desk or in drawingroom, at Solferino's or in Sussex, Henley was constantly "at his best." For, though his turbulency of speech might belie the fact, these were his halcyon days. Publicly he wielded over keen young minds an influence second to no man's in his generation. Privately he was glad almost to the point of tears in his home and family. In Addiscombe Anna, the Châtelaine, graciously received his friends and protégés. Here at Sunday *soirées*, the Regatta renewed their Thursday debates in sessions so strenuous that the Russian Nihilist, Sergius Stepniak, could "not go more than once a year—it [was] too exhausting."[26] But Henley at home was not always the belligerent warrior; he was ever willing in the presence of his little daughter to forget his besetting literary quarrels, content to subordinate his own militant intellect to her matchless serenity. By strange command Margaret ruled the household, like a visiting fairy princess, a child as ethereal in her charm as the Wendy of *Peter Pan* whose character she suggested.[27] "There was," Barrie wrote, "an exuberance of vitality about her as if she

[25] Pennell, *Joseph Pennell*, i, 248, and *Nights*, p. 137.
[26] See Yeats, p. 112.
[27] See Barrie, *Greenwood Hat*, p. 195; and *cf.* James A. Roy, *James Matthew Barrie* (New York, 1938), p. 141.

lived too quickly in her gladness."[28] In her Henley saw incarnate all his own intrinsic gentleness, all the tender sentiment which as editor and critic he felt compelled to suppress.

THE *National Observer* marks the pinnacle of Henley's journalistic achievement. And in point of contributors alone the paper retains a high place among the great Victorian literary weeklies. Apart from ephemeral, though well-written political "leaders" by Greenwood or Whibley or Eustace Balfour, it printed such documents as Stevenson's public correspondence concerning Father Damien, prose pieces of topical interest, which were yet of perdurable value. In its columns appeared familiar essays by Andrew Lang and short stories by J. M. Barrie. Joseph Pennell contributed articles on the technique of etching. And William Archer and A. B. Walkley reviewed the renascent drama; while Stéphane Mallarmé sent spirited accounts in French of *premières* at Parisian playhouses. Nor was the poetry published in the journal less distinguished than the prose. Cosmo Monkhouse, Katharine de Mattos, Graham Tomson, Edmund Gosse, and A. Mary F. Robinson all performed competently within the narrow confines of society verse; Alfred Austin seemed less than usually bathetic when confined to the sonnet-form; and Swinburne accommodated himself with ease to his own roundel-pattern. But there were other and more original voices. Alice Meynell struck a deep note of passionate Catholicism; and T. E. Brown intoned the strenuously acceptant philosophy, mellowed but unshadowed by time, that years before had endeared him to a Gloucester schoolboy. Henley himself chanted in new free rhythms the *London Voluntaries*; and Rudyard Kipling sang the *Barrack Room Ballads* in a new accent, a Cockney accent, with

[28] See Roy, p. 142. Margaret also appears as Reddy in *Sentimental Tommy*, where Henley is Reddy's author-father "whose beard licked the table while he wrote."

a dramatic immediacy that the Rhymers of the Cheshire Cheese might well have envied. From across the world came the nostalgic last verses of R. L. S.; and out of the Celtic twilight rose the plaintive cries of Katharine Tynan and many lyrics, including "The Lake Isle of Innisfree," softly "tenored" by the young Yeats. The *Yellow Book* at its best never assembled talents richer or more varied.

Though he regretted Henley's militant Conservatism, C. F. G. Masterman could always affectionately remember the "Imperial Review": "What a feast of good things was represented by the old *National Observer*! For a Saturday's sixpence one could obtain the first work of a dozen original and daring minds."[29] And Wilfred Whitten recalled no less vividly his early appreciation of the *Observer*: "What a bliss it struck upon the week! . . . How we shouted and wrote each other notes about Mrs. Meynell's 'Rejection' and Mr. Kenneth Grahame's 'Orion' and Kipling's 'Tomlinson,' and the trail of Henley over all."[30] Other young men with literary ambitions, Ernest Rhys, Maurice Baring, Randall Blackshaw, F. H. Lacon-Watson, and Arthur Waugh were of one mind as to the brilliance of Henley's paper. Nevertheless, for all the enthusiasm it aroused in the apprentice-writer, the *National Observer*, like *London* and the *Magazine of Art*, failed utterly to attract the common reader; no single issue, whatever its wealth of talent or distinction of style, sold more than a thousand copies.[31] Masterman felt that the journal had died of its own overvitality. "The cleverness and originality," he said, "were too naked and unashamed. Men reeled back into the sobriety of *The Spectator* and similar safe periodicals." There was undoubtedly some truth in this explanation of the incredibly bad sales; for if Henley's conversation had

[29] C. F. G. Masterman, *In Peril of Change* (New York, 1905), p. 40.
[30] Quoted by Viola Meynell, *Alice Meynell* (New York, 1929), p. 73.
[31] See Arthur Waugh, *One Man's Road* (London, 1931), p. 247.

155

proved too exhausting for an anarchist's endurance, the prose he published was scarcely calculated to act as sedative upon the comfortable bourgeois mind. But the real cause of unpopularity lay deeper than any mere method of presentation; it was inherent in the editor's attitude towards his reading public.

In November, 1892, Coventry Patmore wrote to Henley a letter of protest concerning the subject-matter of the *National Observer*. Though he could in some respects greatly admire the paper, there was, he regretted to say, almost always in it at least one article, which it had been "at once unwise in the interests of the Paper, and more than dubious in those of good taste and fair morals, to admit." Since Mrs. Patmore and her daughters were, after all, "only decent Englishwomen," it would henceforth, he felt, be necessary to exclude the *Observer* from their home at Lymington. As for Henley's poems, he would admit "their vigour and novelty," though he could not but deplore "their peculiar and . . . uneconomical allusions to sex."

Henley acknowledged the complaint with much respect and a touch of gentle irony. "I am very sorry indeed," he said, "that the N.O. is no longer to be read *chez vous*. But perhaps I could have looked for nothing else." The objectionable article was probably "an error in taste, but the error of an exquisite artist *à ses heures*," and the blame, if any, should fall upon the editor rather than upon the author. In conclusion, he could only add that he was "rather sorry for Lymington this week. For Greenwood (once more with us) [was] in his best form, and Blank and Dash and Three Stars and the others [were] 'equal to themselves!!' "[32]

Thus, while he admired the classic restraint of Patmore's *Unknown Eros*, Henley refused to cater to the respectability of "decent Englishwomen." He bemoaned the fact "that the theory and practice of British art

[32] See Basil Champneys, ed., *Memoirs and Correspondence of Coventry Patmore*, 2 vols. (London, 1900), ii, 272, 393-94.

[were] subject to the influence of the British schoolgirl, and that he [was] unworthy the name of artist whose achievement [was] of a kind to call a blush to the cheek of youth." Sex, he declared, was "the great subject, the leaven of imaginative art."[33] And whatever the false delicacy of his readers, he could not eliminate from his paper the aesthetic treatment of sexual problems. One of his henchmen tells us how the circulation of the *New Review* "dropped like a stone," when there appeared in it "a story . . . in which the seduction of a housemaid was described in fuller detail than was perhaps usual at the time."[34] Henley was not unconcerned with an increase or decrease in the sales of his journal; for on its success or failure his livelihood depended. But he was much more vitally concerned with the autonomy of the artist; and he declined to allow the standards of a merely conventional morality to circumscribe the creative talents of his contributors. When the *Graphic* shrank from printing the christening scene in Hardy's *Tess*, Henley accepted it for publication in the *Observer*.[35] If his defiance of popular taste cost him dearly in subscribers, his uncompromise with Philistinism alone could satisfy his editorial integrity. And in the particular instance of *Tess*, it preserved for all time one of the strongest passages in Victorian fiction.

It was not only in deference to Coventry Patmore that Henley was willing to assume personal responsibility for the subject-matter to which the ladies of Lymington objected. For to a remarkable degree all that Henley published was his own work. "I am glad you like the journal," he told Theodore Watts-Dunton; "I confess that I look upon it with a certain pride. It costs me much time, pains, and invention; but it's worth it, I think. At all events, it is a pleasure to make a good

[33] *Works*, IV, 51, 39.
[34] Herbert Stephen, *London Mercury*, XIII (1926), 399.
[35] See Florence Hardy, *Thomas Hardy*, 2 vols. (London, 1933), I, 315.

number."[36] Whatever he included in the *Observer*, he first assimilated to a preconceived pattern. Through much time, pains, and invention, he achieved for his paper a distinct unity of personality; in the finished product, the "good number," the "trail of Henley" spread "over all." A considerable volume of the unsigned prose and verse came from his own facile pen and naturally bore the stamp of his own style. The authorship of the entertaining articles on ladies' fashion, for instance, could not long remain a mystery to anyone familiar with the manner of the *Views and Reviews*[37]:

> It will be interesting to see how the revival of *Charles I* at the Lyceum is going to affect the season's modes. *Faust* (or perhaps it would be better to say Gretchen) gave us the accordeon skirt; and *Ravenswood* is responsible for the basque, which may yet be superseded (for the year is young) by the debonair elegance, the flowing lines, the brocades and laces, of an earlier and better-dressed day. . . . Provided your effect comply on broad lines with contemporary convention, you may practically wear what you like. And this not after the manner of the Ibsenites and Socialists (they were called Aesthetes of old), but so gracefully and unpretentiously as to achieve the Golden Mean between modishness and originality.[38]

Henley's style, vivid, incisive, ironic, infected the writing of each Regatta member who, self-consciously, and with Henley's encouragement, strove to equal the master's prose. But whenever one of the "Young Men" or one of the "Signing Contributors" failed to conform to the editor's theory of composition, the editor felt obliged, always in the interests of "rhythm," to make necessary emendations. Into a Shavian eulogy of Mozart he interpolated abuse of Wagner in order to achieve antithetical

---

[36] Thomas Hake and Arthur Compton-Rickett, *The Life and Letters of Theodore Watts-Dunton*, 2 vols. (London, 1916), II, 71.

[37] Any mystery there might be is dispelled by contemporary evidence; see unsigned note, *Critic*, XXXI (1897), 367.

[38] *NO*, v, 429.

balance; and it was, as the "perfect Wagnerite" remarked, exceedingly characteristic of him not to understand why he had lost his contributor.[39] More submis-
sive than Shaw, truly glad that any fragment of his work
could find a publisher, Yeats resigned himself to the revision of his lyrics; "I was comforted," he explained, "by
my belief that [Henley] also rewrote Kipling then in
the first flood of popularity."[40] Mrs. Pennell who contributed notes on continental cookery was perplexed
rather than annoyed at the merciless editing; when her
articles appeared in print, it was, she said, "an open
question with [her] whether [she] had the right to call
them [hers] and to take any money for them."[41] Laud-
able or not, Henley's editorial practice accomplished
the desired effect. His paper not by accident attained
its uniformity of excellence. With clear thinking and
crisp writing, it countered the rococo prose of an aesthetic "decadence." Deliberately, it "taught incisiveness
to a generation prone to lose itself in words."[42]

In manner and matter the *National Observer* served
as a protest against Victorian journalism. And like all
fresh protests, its appeal was frankly esoteric; none but
the most determined modernist could appreciate its aim
and achievement. Its trenchant epigram and startling
paradox made flagrant demand upon the reader's mental
agility; and its persistent satire unsettled approved
ideals. Thoroughly iconoclastic, its most brilliant reviews conveyed the impression that society was entirely
degenerate and that the latest books written about it
had no excuse for existence. Indeed, in one issue, the
editor prefixed a note to the department of current
literature declaring: "The state of the publishing trade
is such that, for this week at least, we can give reviews
of old books alone: done, it is right to say, in several

[39] See Henderson, *Shaw*, p. 212.
[40] Yeats, p. 113. Kipling's "popularity" is doubtful; see Henley's
comment, quoted above, p. 135, n.
[41] Pennell, *Nights*, p. 141.
[42] Hugh Walker, *Cambridge History of English Literature*, xiv, 147.

styles, as though the themes were actual and the authors were of today."[43] Here followed mock-serious reviews of the "classics" approached from diverse points of view. Scott's *Ivanhoe* and Pierce Egan's *Boxiana* might be mentioned as commendable efforts. Lord Byron's *Don Juan* seemed "a good counterpiece to Mr. Hardy's *Tess of the D'Urbervilles,*" insofar as it told "the history of a pure man, . . a Tennysonian King Arthur *manqué*"; but the noble author might improve his rhymes immeasurably, were he to "make a study of the works of Mr. Gosse or some other truly cultivated poet, before he publishe[d] another 'epic.'" James Boswell's *Life of Samuel Johnson* could hastily be dismissed by the reviewer as a "tedious and silly book." The author of *Coningsby* should be warned against modeling himself on the works of Mr. Oscar Wilde. And the poet of *In Memoriam* should be roundly denounced for inventing "a new language, the language of the Sentimental Coward." Each member of the Regatta joined with gusto in the frivolity; each was writing for his fellows, as young, as vivacious as himself; each blithely ignored a larger public which might well misunderstand his vigorous talents. If the device of the retrospective review was confined to a single issue, the attitude of mind that suggested it was the spirit animating the whole periodical throughout its six vital years.

Wilde spoke a larger truth than he knew when he remarked of Henley: "He founded a school and has survived all his disciples."[44] For with the failure of the *National Observer*, the Young Men passed forever beyond Henley's control; each henceforth, if he were to continue at all in the profession of letters, had to find his own style and his own market; no longer could he expect the master's encouragement and criticism; no longer could he depend upon set assignments to be completed for the Thursday galley proofs. Yeats tells of one

[43] *NO*, x, 381.
[44] Quoted by Rothenstein, *Men and Memories*, i, 312.

Young Man who, unable to make the necessary individual adjustment, fell upon evil days; "this young man" had once written "articles and reviews notorious for savage wit; and years afterwards when the *National Observer* was dead, Henley dying, and our cavern of outlaws empty, I met him in Paris very sad and I think very poor. 'Nobody will employ me now,' he said. 'Your master is gone,' I answered, 'and you are like the spear in an old Irish story that had to be kept dipped in poppy-juice that it might not go about killing people on its own account.' "[45] But to those who had relied on Henley for stimulus rather than inspiration, his principles remained valid long after his personal influence had ceased to function. Kipling and Whibley carried his battle into the new century, where they lived to see the defeat of the aesthetic doctrine made final and the victory of neo-realism assured.

[45] Yeats, pp. 112-13.

∝§ CHAPTER 11. "THE WAY OF REALISM." PRINCIPLES OF LITERARY CRITICISM

FROM the Chénier article of 1875 till the essay on *Othello* a few months before his death, Henley clung faithfully to his own critical standards. Chénier he linked to a line of Greek elegiac poets; *Othello* he considered in the light of an Elizabethan convention. Throughout his criticism his method was synthetic rather than analytical; he measured a literary work always in its relation to a literary context and never as an isolated aesthetic event. He was capable of capturing in a few brilliant generalizations the quality of a book or the spirit of an age; but he had neither the patience nor the power to trace to its origins a particular seminal idea or to describe in detail the processes by which a given poem had evolved. Avowedly "no metaphysician,"[1] he had no interest in logical deduction from abstract philosophic truth; with an invalid's faith in basic physical sensation, he reasoned empirically towards a coherent universe. By nature he was utterly unable to appreciate a literature of introspection; and all too readily he repudiated the artist wrapt in a contemplation of intangibles as one who sought to evade the realities of his world and his time. Without doubt his failure to achieve full sympathy with creative minds alien to his own placed his criticism under severe limitation. But from this failure alone arose his true significance as a critical force. He came at the close of a troubled era sick from its own doubt, weary of its febrile intellection. Yet once he had learned by painful experience his individual grammar of assent, he could in no way comprehend the Victorian denial, the omnipresent romantic *malaise dans une civilisation*. By an activist ethic he was prepared to accept the diversity of human nature as intrinsically good. Poetry, he said correcting Arnold,

[1] See *Works*, II, 100, n.

was nothing more than an "expression of life."[2] And in life, which meant the free exercise of an unconquerable soul, there was no place for a paralyzing despair.

In its most naïve form, activism led Henley to an admiration of lusty extrovert action as a prime source of literary material. The preface to *A Book of English Prose*, on which he collaborated with Charles Whibley, explained that "since our anthology is for young as well as for old, we have preferred before the prose of reflection and analysis the prose of adventure and romance—surely the best motives for sound and spirited English?"[3] By virtue of an incomparable narrative gusto, Dumas became to him "one of the heroes of modern art," one who remained "to the end a prodigy of force and industry, a miracle of cleverness and accomplishment and ease, a type of generous and abundant humanity, a great artist in many varieties of form, a prince of talkers and story-tellers, one of the kings of the stage, a benefactor of his epoch and his kind."[4] Scott endured, despite a slipshod style, by reason of his delight in active living, "his immense and vivid instinct of the picturesque, his inexhaustible humanity, his magnificent moral health, his abounding and infallible sense of the eternal realities of life."[5] And Tolstoi was redeemed from a regrettable mysticism by his epic portrayal of "the vaster incidents, the more tremendous issues,"[6] of Austerlitz and Borodino and the retreat from Russia. Dumas, Scott, Tolstoi, and the early English prose-masters before them, were all to a degree concerned with heroic values; and it was inevitable that the activist should applaud their effort.[7]

[2] See *Works*, II, 383.

[3] Henley and Whibley, eds., *A Book of English Prose, Character and Incident* (London, 1894), "Preface," p. v.

[4] *Works*, IV, 31. [5] *Works*, IV, 230.

[6] *Works*, IV, 205.

[7] *Cf.* Stevenson's letter to Henley from Hyères, 1883: "Your Dumas I think exquisite; it might even have been stronglier said: the brave old godly pagan, I adore his big footprints on the earth."—Stevenson, *Letters, Works*, XXV, 182.

Henley's "masculine protest," however, expressed itself critically not alone in his enjoyment of robustious elemental action; it had deeper and less direct implications. It brought him into immediate and lasting conflict not merely with the aesthetic "decadence," but also with the ideals and inhibitions of the same society against which the "decadents" themselves were reacting. Throughout his essays and reviews Henley repeatedly assailed Victorianism with all the "vigor" at his command. Against his father's generation and his own, he leveled charges sweeping enough to indict himself. The Victorian age was, he contended, "noisy and affected," with "an element of swagger in all its words and ways" and "a distressing and immoral turn for publicity." Forever "straining after picturesque effects," it had lost "the trick of amenity and good breeding"; and only a rare book like Austin Dobson's *Eighteenth Century Essays* remained to prove that it was still "possible to be eloquent without adjectives and elegant without affectation."[8]

Decent, pharisaical, self-conscious, sentimental, the Victorians, taken by and large, were, as Henley saw them, both intellectually and emotionally dishonest. They had no deep sympathy with their own most candid critics; they were "the reverse of profoundly interested" in Meredith's "savage and scathing attack on the superstitions of respectability"; they all but ignored Arnold when he frankly "told the age its faults and suggested such remedies as the study of great men's work had suggested to him"; they suffered complacently their lack of T. E. Brown's "blessed gift of seeing people as they are and not as they ought to be." Despite his own deliberate mannerism, his "swagger," his overstatement, Henley himself was fundamentally sincere in his revolt against a hollow convention. He was, of course, not alone in his rebellion. But, while the "decadents" sought escape from Victorianism in an unnatural perversion of

[8] See *Works*, IV, 80, 175.

its standards, Henley and his followers attacked an artificial restraint, explicitly in the interests of a sounder
"moral health." The artist, they believed, had the right
and duty to "select" his materials; but the artist who
gingerly avoided certain subjects under taboo was guilty
of unforgivable compromise with reality. Reticence,
when it meant fear to discuss without equivocation the
vital issues of modern life, was in nowise to be condoned.
Sentiment, when it implied the glossing of an ugly truth,
was not only unethical but also inartistic. From first to
last the *National Observer* insisted upon a complete and
disillusioned acceptance of the full experience. And
from first to last in his own criticism Henley decried
every evidence of hypocrisy, evasion, and obscurantism.
His dissatisfaction with Victorian social morality induced him to praise and to publish the forbidden chapter of Hardy's *Tess.* And his righteous indignation at
what seemed wilful distortion of fact prompted his
notorious attack on the official biography of "Lewis"
Stevenson. "I read," he said, "and as I read I am op-
pressed by the thought that here is Lewis Stevenson
very much as he may well have wanted to be, but that
here is not Lewis Stevenson at all. . . . I take a view
of Stevenson which is my own, and which declines to
be concerned with this Seraph in Chocolate, this barley-
sugar effigy of a real man; . . the Shorter Catechist of
Vailima, however brilliant and distinguished as a writer
of stories, however authorised and acceptable as an
artist in morals, is not my old, riotous, intrepid, scornful
Stevenson at all."[9]
Recognizing the validity of Henley's charge, Stevenson's later biographers have been at some pains to dis-
credit the legend of R. L. S. But to Henry James, and
to all who were intent upon preserving intact the gentility of Louis, the criticism seemed merely an "overflow
of Henley's gall, . . really rather a striking and lurid—
and so far interesting case—of long discomfortable jeal-

[9] "R. L. S.," *Pall Mall Magazine,* xxv (1901), 505, 508.

ousy and ranklement turned at last to a posthumous (as it were!) malignity, and making the man do, *coram publico*, his ugly act, risking the dishonour for the assuagement."[10] For his courage in speaking his mind, and in so exposing himself to Jamesian disapproval, Henley suffered much, *coram publico*, before a most respectable jury. But it was through his consistent honesty of outlook that he impressed his Regatta and won his influence. Long before the Stevenson article, one of the Young Men had written admiringly of him as "beyond question the most formidable presence in English letters today," a critic whose "authority has slowly undermined the prestige of middle-Victorian ideals."[11] As far as his own circle was concerned, his repudiation of Victorianism carried complete conviction. But iconoclasm alone could not serve him as a sound basis for critical theory. When he found the older ideals, aesthetic or moral, no longer tenable, he was driven to seek other and ampler standards of judgment.

The aesthetes from the Swinburne of *Poems and Ballads* to the Wilde of *Salomé* turned in their reaction to Victorian art towards the literature of France. Henley himself had learned much concerning the discipline of metre from the fifteenth century formalists and from the Parnassians of the Second Empire. He had studied and imitated the technique of French romantic drama. He had introduced to an English public the work of the pre-impressionist French painters. And—what is more relevant to a discussion of his literary criticism— he had read deeply in Sainte-Beuve and Taine and had examined the first principles of contemporary French "realism." It was to be expected then that he should draw from the disillusioned Frenchmen support for his campaign against "middle-Victorian" sentimentalism.

[10] James, *Letters*, I, 386; James admits that he has not read the article! But Colvin and Gosse similarly deplored the attack. Chesterton was one of the few who agreed with Henley that Balfour's biography was inadequate.

[11] H. B. Marriott-Watson, *Bookman*, II (1895), 186.

Nevertheless, on due consideration of the Flaubertian "realist's" claim to an honest portrayal of reality, he rejected the theory of art as incompatible with an activist's philosophy of life. For the "realist" proved hardly less inhibited than the sentimentalist and certainly more distrustful of high passion; while he laid a rightful emphasis on the clutch of circumstance, he failed to consider the individual's resistance to his fell destiny; there was no place in his factualism for "the expression of human feeling in the coil of a tragic situation."[12] Whereas Balzac, working from experience, had achieved "the heroic aggrandizement of things trivial," Champfleury contented "himself with observing and noting and reflecting; with making prose prosaic and adding sobriety and plainness to a plain and sober story; with being merely curious and intelligent; . . with considering fact not as the raw material of inspiration but as inspiration itself."[13] Moreover, the objectivity of the French "realists" was more theoretical than actual; for there was in Flaubert a sadism which engendered a perverse delight in the grotesquerie of *Salammbô*; and Zola was vitiated throughout by a "barren pessimism" which beclouded his whole presentation of human society.[14] Tolstoi was a "realist" of a different mold; his was "not the realism of externals and trivial details—though of this there [was] enough for art if not for the common Zolaphyte—but the higher and better sort, the realism which [dealt] with mental and spiritual conditions, the realism of *Othello* and *Hamlet*."[15] Yet the "realism" of Tolstoi, like that of Balzac, was too individual to be set up as a model for imitation, too much a product of one man's abundant creative genius to serve as a touchstone of judgment. The true antithesis to the doctrine of Flaubert and the example of Zola lay in the theory and

[12] *Works*, IV, 46.   [13] *Works*, IV, 135-36.
[14] See *Works*, IV, 58, 204, 209. Henley makes no sharp distinction between French "realism" and French "naturalism."
[15] *Works*, IV, 203.

practice of the British "realists" of the eighteenth century, who had all the blessed gift of seeing things as they are. And in the work of these Henley found the most effective antidote to the denial, the sentimentalism, and the false respectability of his own time.

The Victorian revival of the eighteenth century seemed to Henley on a par with the discovery of Japan. As the aesthetes ignored the underlying symbolism of Oriental art to admire a mere arrangement of line and color, so the antiquarian valued the superficial graces of the Augustan age to the exclusion of its true character. "What attracts us," Henley wrote, "is its outside. We are in love with its houses and its china and its costumes. We are not enamoured of it as it was but as it seems to Mr. Caldecott and Mr. Dobson and Miss Kate Greenaway. . . . Our love is not for the essentials of the time but only for its accidents and oddities; and we express it in pictures and poems and fantasies in architecture, and the canonisation (in figures) of Chippendale and Sheraton. But it is questionable if we might not with advantage increase our interest, and carry imitation a little deeper."[16]

In the course of his own deeper researches into the actual culture of the eighteenth century, Henley asked exactly how "classical"—in the Graeco-Roman sense of the word—was the English "classical" period. To him the best of Georgian writing, whatever its formal derivations from ancient literature, was rooted in an Anglo-Saxon tradition; Defoe and Swift and Fielding concerned themselves not less than Chaucer with a frank depiction of the manners and morals of contemporary English society. All were "realists" in their honest regard for the realities of human experience. Indeed the one essential characteristic of the eighteenth century poets and novelists seemed to be their utter honesty of vision. Smollett's cynicism might be discomforting; but it was marked by a sincerity towards which Thackeray,

[16] *Works*, IV, 173-74.

the major Victorian cynic, could never attain; Smollett
was "indecent naturally, yet deliberately: indecent because he must be, but also because he will"; and there
was more genuine cynicism in a single Smollett character than in "all the sentimental carpings of the Middle-
Victorian moralist."[17] If absolute sincerity could make
of the pessimist an artist, it showed to even better advantage in the work of one who was by nature more
cheerful in his acceptance of reality. Through his hearty
joy in the life about him and his consummate power of
expression, Fielding became to Henley "our premier
novelist," "a great and good man, who also, by premedi-
tation and design, laboriously created an Art, and created it in such terms, and to such a purpose, that none
has practised it since his time but must have worked
and written differently if this immortal Master had not
written and worked before him."[18] Among Fielding's
admirers, Henley was, according to a recent scholar,
"not only most eloquent but most intuitively just"; and
Henley's preface to the complete works "marked an
epoch in Fielding's fame; it put the stamp of its author's
authority upon an admirable general estimate of Fielding's genius and it severely arraigned his predecessors
for their delinquencies."[19] Austin Dobson, the soundest
of the earlier critics, had been "rather more apologetical"
than he needed to be and also "somewhat Middle-Victorian in mood and effect."[20] But to Henley, Fielding's
fiction required no such apologist; his realistic novel,
throbbing with life and vigor, was its own advocate:
"Which is to be pitied? The artist of *Amelia* and *Jona-
than Wild*, the creator of the Westerns and Parson
Adams and Colonel Bath? or we the whipper-snappers
of sentiment—the critics who can neither read nor understand?"[21]

[17] *Works*, ii, 93.   [18] *Works*, ii, 46.
[19] Frederic T. Blanchard, *Fielding the Novelist* (New Haven, 1927),
pp. 517, 518.
[20] *Works*, ii, 5.   [21] *Works*, iv, 211.

In the longest of his eighteenth century studies Henley appraised the life and work of Robert Burns, the poet of "realism," whom the whippersnappers of sentiment had thoroughly misread and misunderstood. Now usually regarded as his finest critical work, the *Essay on Burns* proved, on its appearance in 1897, the most provocative literary biography of the period.[22] Ardent Burnsites from Kilmarnock to San Francisco decried the temerity of the "penurious Cockney," the "popularity-seeking and shilling-hunting biographer," whose "superficial summing up of the environment of Burns [partook] more of the nature of a national libel than an attack on the personality of the Bard."[23] These repudiations were gathered together by one John D. Ross under the title, *Henley and Burns, or the Critic Censured* "being a collection of papers replying to an offensive critique on the life, genius, and achievements of the Scottish Poet." Denouncing Henley's "appreciation" as "that most unsavoury piece of criticism—that blot upon literature," Ross found "one redeeming feature about the *Essay* and only one—it was not written by a Scotsman. Thank Heaven for that! No countryman of Burns could be guilty of laying such filth before the world." The *Greenock Telegraph* for January 24, 1898, demanded:

> Why should Carlyle's life have been held up to the world by Froude, and Burns by Henley? Is it because they were divinely gifted Scotsmen? . . . Is the exposure of human foibles particularly gratifying to some English natures?

[22] Raleigh disagreed with Henley concerning Burns's private life, though he felt Henley a juster critic than Stevenson; see Raleigh, *Letters*, 2 vols. (London, 1928), II, 525. D. H. Lawrence wrote from Italy in 1913 praising Henley's essay; see Lawrence, *Letters* (New York, 1932), p. 94. John Buchan called Henley's "the fullest and on the whole the fairest estimate" of Burns; see complete *Burns* (London, 1926), p. xi. Franklyn Bliss Snyder quarrels with Henley's view of Burns's love life, calls essay "brilliant but misleading"; see Snyder, *Robert Burns* (New York, 1932), p. 355.
[23] John D. Ross, ed., *Henley and Burns* (London, 1901), pp. 105, 38, 25.

Despite his name, John S. Macnab was more objective in his attack on the *Essay*; lamenting "the New Realism in criticism," he conceded that "Mr. Henley is spoken of in London as a master prose writer and as a well-known poet, and by admiring friends as a 'princely critic' of modern art and literature." Two generations later when the methods of "the New Realism" have become standard technique in literary criticism, it is difficult to see wherein the *Essay* could have offended. A certain Mr. F. Faithfull Begg, M. P., represented in the *Henley and Burns* collection, inadvertently provides a clue in his defense of "those middle-class virtues which Mr. Henley considered such contemptible things." As the defense implies, Henley had measured Burns by his own scale of values rather than by any respectable Victorian standard. In fact, he had explicitly declared his approach:

> As for reading [Burns's writings] in Victorian terms—Early-Victorian terms or Late—that way madness lies; madness, and a Burns that by no process known to gods or men could ever have existed save in the lubber-land of some Pious Editor's dream.[24]

A resolution to consider all the facts, even those not usually discussed, underlay Henley's unretouched portrait of the earthy Scot who prided himself on his illegitimate children. Yet this "debunking" was positive rather than negative in intention; it was designed to rescue Burns from the moral prude who delighted in the sententious "Cotter's Saturday Night," a poem "doomed to popularity from the first; being of its essence sentimental and therefore pleasingly untrue, and being, also of its essence, patriotic—an assertion of the honour and the glory and the piety of Scotland." For "the sincere and abounding humour" and "the plenitude of life . . . of the early pieces in the Vernacular," Henley had none but the highest praise, praise which as a matter of course

24 *Works*, ii, 142.

implied a derogation of Victorian poetry. "Such attempts at reconstruction as *The Earthly Paradise* and *The Idylls of the King* will," he said, " 'fade far away, dissolve,' and be quite forgotten, ere these pictures disfeature or dis-limn." For Burns "had the good sense to concern himself with the life he knew. The way of realism lay broad-beaten by his ancestors, and was natural to his feet."

"The way of realism," the path of honest acceptance and universal sympathy—herein lay for the activist the one possible approach to a sound philosophy of life. Yet the interests of "Life," of the continuous process of growth and decay, were scarcely identical with the interests of "Art," of completed patterns which allowed no continuum beyond themselves. From the outset, therefore, Henley found himself as critic of literature faced with the conflict between art and reality. At times he might make pretense of denying the conflict altogether, by relegating art to an entirely subordinate position; "Byron and Burns," he once wrote, "courted Life like a mistress, and made no more account of Art than many make of their wives, but were satisfied with companionship, and a pleasant house, and the presence of a goodly and fruitful issue."[25] But his own work was sufficient proof that he could seldom follow Byron and Burns in taking art so for granted. Throughout his highly polished verse and prose he remained forever the deliberate craftsman, the self-conscious stylist.

To Henley the "realism" of the eighteenth century implied much more than a mere transcript of observable natural phenomena. Reality, he declared, was "but the beginning, the raw material of art." The aesthetic value of a literary work depended on the author's ability "to select and to inspire the results of his selection."[26] Contrary to common opinion, Boswell achieved the supreme biography not through accident, but through his mastery

[25] Henley, ed., *The Poetry of Wilfrid Blunt* (London, 1898), Preface, p. viii.
[26] *Works*, IV, 163, 164.

"of selection, composition, and design; of the art of working a large number of essential details into a uniform and living whole."[27] But facts alone, however skillfully arranged, did not procure this "living" aesthetic unity. For art was primarily a form of individual expression rather than a means of impersonal exposition. And it was through its "passionate human quality," through the artist's understanding of the life he sought to portray, that a great book accomplished its effect as a moral agent. Boswell shaped "the results of his selection" with a genuine feeling for his subject, and Tolstoi molded his chronicle of conquest and defeat with his own "persuasive and inspiring" faith in the eternal resurgence of the human spirit. The subject itself did not much matter as long as the artist brought to it a sound emotional instinct and a healthy sense of proportion. Both *Pamela* and *Joseph Andrews*, for instance, treated of "Fornication, the Sole Unpardonable Sin in English Fiction"; but in Fielding's novel, fornication was "but a detail (as it is in life)," whereas in *Pamela* it was "the staple of the book"—

> Mr. B. is always hovering round in a most dreadful and indecent state; and Pamela is always praying to be protected from a kind of Walking Phallus (as in a Kaulbach allegory), terribly menacing and ever ineffectual, or resisting its approaches, or writing to her parents to tell them that it has had no luck, and that she is still their Virgin child. Which is the more moral writer? Which the more buxom book?[28]

Fielding, then, was admirable as a writer who had frankly assessed human nature in all its diversity and recorded his judgment with matchless humor and wholehearted sincerity. Richardson, on the other hand, was contemptible as one who had mistaken a single aspect of experience for its sum total and reproduced it with

---

[27] "Boswell," *Works*, IV, 180. Henley is, I believe, the first critic to take a thoroughly sympathetic attitude towards Boswell's "art."
[28] *Works*, II, 40, n.

"a new-fangled blend of sentimental priggishness and prurient unreality."[29]

In such criticism Henley approached a moral standard comparable to Ruskin's ideal of Purity. And in general Henley stood closer to the "middle-Victorian" aesthetician than he would ever have admitted. Like Ruskin, he believed that art was essentially a means of communication, that there existed between artist and spectator a bond of sympathy whereby an emotion might be passed from the creative to the receptive mind. The greatest and the most moral artist was he who saw deepest into the wholeness of things.[30] And the greatest art was consequently that which showed the truest correspondence with reality and gave the best evidence of the creator's power of interpretation. Victor Hugo's work was to Henley but an expression of Hugo's fundamental insincerity, of his moral insufficiency, for "all his life long he was addicted to attitude; all his life long he was a *poseur* of the purest water." By such affectation Hugo's verses were vitiated beyond redemption; though the poet "had the genius of style in such fulness as entitles him to rank with the great artists in words of all time," his best lyrics were merely trivial; they were "not necessaries but luxuries"; and life could continue very well without them.[31]

As the artist was to interpret "human nature in its fulness," so should the critic interpret the finished art-product with a thorough understanding of its "intention" and a complete realization of its "effect." He must appreciate to the full the possibilities of the chosen aesthetic medium. Fielding's *Tom Jones*, for example, was a first-rate novel; but judged by dramatic standards, it proved a work immeasurably inferior to Vanbrugh's *Provok'd Wife*, for over against the speech of

29 *Works*, IV, 196.
30 *Cf*. Ruskin, "Human Nature in its fulness is necessarily moral."
—*Works*, 39 vols. (Library Edition, London, 1903-1912), XXXIII, 173.
31 See Henley, *Works*, IV, 63-69.

Squire Western, Henley could place the talk of Sir John
Brute, which was "stuff done for the Stage for the very
simple reason that it could not possibly, any more than
Othello and *Hamlet* could, be done for anything else."[32]
In literature, then, as in painting, it was essential that
artist or critic be familiar with the conventions of his
chosen genre. Accepting this prerequisite, we may per-
tinently remark that the authors of *Deacon Brodie* and
Beau Austin, had they made finer distinction between
fictional and dramatic technique, might more deeply
have influenced the English theater.

"The Poet," said Henley, "springs from a compost of
ideals and experiences and achievements, whose essences he absorbs and assimilates, and in whose absence
he could not be a Poet."[33] And the poem, therefore, or
the novel, or the drama, springs from a definite social
and aesthetic milieu which plays no small part in de-
termining its form and content. The Regency was

> a dreadful age, no doubt: for all its solid foundations,
> of faith and dogma in the Church and of virtue and sol-
> vency in the State, a fierce, drunken, gambling, "keep-
> ing," adulterous, high-living, hard-drinking, hard-hit-
> ting, brutal age. But it was Byron's; and *Don Juan* and
> *The Giaour* are as naturally its outcomes as *Absalom
> and Achitophel* is an expression of the Restoration, and
> *In Memoriam* a product of Victorian England.[34]

Whether he spoke for an age or for all time, Shakespeare himself could not be wholly isolated from the
ideals and achievements of his own generation. From
first to last, Henley insisted, his art was subject not only
to the general conventions of the dramatic method but
to the specific conditions of the Elizabethan theater. It
was probable that the very characters of Richard and
Hamlet and Lear had been adapted to the peculiar talents of Burbage. It was certain that the dramatist wrote
with a direct regard for the taste of his audience. Such

[32] *Works*, II, 24-25.   [33] *Works*, II, 159.
[34] *Works*, II, 263-64.

an approach to Shakespearean scholarship must have savored of heresy at a time when A. C. Bradley was preparing the most eloquent of many "romantic" appreciations. Anticipating the "realist" critics by many years, Henley argued that *Othello* was not to be read in terms of modern psychology but rather in the light of a dramatic theory by which the structure of a play depended on a variation in emotional tensions.[35]

In this emphasis on convention and environment we may trace a probable derivation from Taine's theory of the milieu as a major conditioning factor in an aesthetic development. To the influence of Taine may also be ascribed Henley's concern with the artist's peculiar attribute, his *faculté maîtresse*, the cast of mind or flair for technique that gave his work its distinctive flavor. Cyril Tourneur, for instance, who stemmed from Shakespeare's milieu but who lacked Shakespeare's breadth and depth of genius, yet retained a place in literature by force of his "master quality," the talent for vitalizing words with passion, the "power of so charging a phrase with energy and colour as to make it convey the emotion of the writer at the instant of inspiration."[36] Like Taine, Henley believed that it was the critic's function to discover and describe the master quality of the artist in a given art-object. Now the discovery itself entailed a prerequisite critical endowment. In finding the quintessence of a book, mere scholarship divorced from intuition counted for little; "academic persons," more gifted with patience than insight, were "things made after supper at the Muses' table out of a melon rind."[37] Nevertheless, conjoined to a sympathetic understanding of the creative process, research into the particular circumstances

[35] See *Works*, II, 364-76. Henley's essay appeared in 1903; Bradley's *Shakespearean Tragedy*, in 1904. *Cf.* Elmer Edgar Stoll's acknowledgment that Henley "presents a conception of tragedy, similar, even in phrasing and figure, to mine."—*Shakespeare and Other Masters* (Cambridge, Mass., 1940), p. 52.

[36] *Works*, IV, 96.

[37] *Works*, II, 385.

of aesthetic production might enormously enrich the
critic's power of judgment.

Despite his gusto of manner, his penchant for sweeping generalization, his habit of quoting and misquoting
from memory, Henley himself displayed throughout his
criticism an almost incredible erudition. Having read
and assimilated the masterpieces of five languages, English, French, German, Italian, and Spanish, he brought
to his essays and reviews an admirable capacity for comparative estimates. He made himself thoroughly familiar
with the best that earlier critics had thought and said,
and so prepared himself intelligently to refute any opinions that ran counter to his own conviction. Since he
felt that biographical data might illuminate the character and intention of the author, he saturated himself
in memoirs, diaries, and commonplace books; as a result, his monograph on Smollett revealed a firsthand
knowledge of eighteenth century literary quarrels; and
his survey of "Byron's World," though written entirely
without notes,[38] betrayed a truly encyclopaedic command of Regency gossip. His shorter literary *aperçus*
brilliantly measured each author against the other artists in his genre; a single paragraph "placed" Longfellow
among the great sea poets; and a page served to touch
off Balzac's unique contribution to European letters. His
longer critical essays made deeper incursions into the
backgrounds out of which the writer under scrutiny had
emerged; the memorable Burns edition implied a detailed knowledge of countless minor dialect poets; and
the sketch of Henry Fielding's career rested, in part at
least, upon an examination of the record-books of the
Old Bailey sessions.[39] But in all his studies, short or long,
erudite or simply intuitive, Henley's first purpose was
the discernment of the individuality stamped by the artist upon the matter of his creation.

The description of a master quality presented as many

[38] This was Henley's boast; see Cornford, *Henley*, p. 54.
[39] See *Works*, ii, 43, n.

problems as its detection. Though well able to express his judgments in direct expository prose, Henley preferred a more dramatic critical method. In his terse *Views and Reviews* he strove to reduce his literary estimates to single impressions such as might be passed on to the reader in a handful of shining epigrams: Congreve was "the laureate of a generation that was only alive for half an hour in the course of all the twenty-four"; George Meredith wrote "with the pen of a great artist in his left hand and the razor of a spiritual suicide in his right"; Heine "had a light hand with the branding-iron and marked his subjects not more neatly than indelibly"; and "the Muse of M. de Banville was born not naked but in the most elaborate and sumptuous evening wear that ever muse put on." "Your true essayist," said Henley, ". . . must be personal, or his hearers can feel no manner of interest in him."[40] Yet it is a defect of Henley's own essays that much of the vivid impressionism seems too personal, too arbitrary, to have a firm objective basis. Invariably stimulating, his epigrams seldom appear other than brilliant impromptus; they indicate little of the careful consideration and genuine literary insight that went into their manufacture.

But the epigrammatic technique by no means accounts for the whole of Henley's critical method. The impressionism is counterbalanced by what might be called "expressionism"; and this of its nature implies a deliberately impersonal approach to the art-object. By expressionism, Henley attempted to identify himself completely with the author's mind and thereby to re-create the author's world. "In Herrick," he wrote, "the air is fragrant with new-mown hay; there is a morning light upon all things; long shadows streak the grass, and on the eglantine swinging in the hedge the dew lies white and brilliant."[41] As the "Herrick" recaptured the very physical sensations of the pastoral poet, so the re-

[40] *Works*, iv, 172.   [41] *Works*, iv, 101.

construction of the *Arabian Nights Entertainments* distilled the atmosphere itself of the spiced groves of sandalwood and cedar:

> The sea-horse ramps at [the heroes] from the ocean floor; the great roc darkens earth about them with the shadow of his wings; wise and goodly apes come forth and minister unto them; enchanted camels bear them over evil deserts with the swiftness of the wind, or the magic horse outspreads his sail-broad vannes, and soars with them; or they are borne aloft by some servant of the Spell till the earth is as a bowl beneath them, and they hear the angels quiring at the foot of the Throne. . . .[42]

In such passages the poet and the critic were at one; the literature that struck a responsive chord in his mind became to Henley a present reality and so the actual stuff of inspiration. Through expressionism he achieved his strongest effects; so fully realized were his empathic judgments that there seemed nothing of subjective caprice in them.

In point of technique, Henley's literary criticism was not unlike that of Walter Pater, whose appreciations most fully had exploited the expressionistic method. Both critics approached a work of art with the bias of the individualist. Each evolved for his own use a highly personal style; Pater's prose moved by exquisite delays through long-lingering periods; Henley's bristled with paradox and oxymoron, with sharp epigram and explosive epithet. And each sought for the distinctive trait, the master quality, of the author he would judge. But Pater's individualism was the philosophy of the aesthete who asked of art a refuge from the social conflict; whereas Henley's was the credo of the activist who felt a physical and moral duty strenuously to exercise his own soul in "the brave gymnasium" of time. The one doctrine was destined, even in spite of its teacher, to inspire the literature of "decadence." The other served as a basis for Edwardian realism.

[42] *Works*, IV, 189.

Whether or not they had been exposed to the personal influence of Henley, the major post-Victorians, Chesterton, Conrad, Kipling, Bennett, Galsworthy, Wells, were all to a degree conditioned by the revolt against aestheticism. And in their search for new standards they gained not a little from the revival of the eighteenth century, in which Henley had played a dominant role. They had read Flaubert and Taine with sympathy and understanding; and yet in their own work they were "realists" with a difference. Chesterton's essays recaptured the common-sensical humor of Dr. Johnson, the cheerful, half-ironic optimism of Fielding. And *The Old Wives' Tale*, for all its French derivation, was permeated with an English faith in the indomitable individual will; Samuel Povey, unlike M. Homais, died "a very honest man," one who displayed at the last "the vein of greatness which runs through every soul without exception." It had been Henley's place to guide Chesterton and Bennett and the younger generation as a whole away from Gallic pessimism, towards a more robust acceptance of reality; it had been his function to reassert the fundamental heroic human values at a time when the sanctions behind them seemed rapidly to be crumbling. That these values were of prime significance as the basis of aesthetic expression, the Edwardian achievement in character-portrayal stands as sufficient proof. The fact that the neo-Georgian artist has repudiated them and so has sacrificed claim to a depiction of the whole truth, this is evidence only of their permanent validity.

PART V. CREATIVE PATTERNS

Ich blick' in die Ferne,
Ich seh' in der Näh
Den Mond und die Sterne
Den Wald und das Reh. . . .
Ihr glücklichen Augen
Was je ihr gesehn,
Es sei wie es wolle,
Es war doch so schön.

—FAUST, II

Long after the Regatta had disbanded, Henley was
left to ponder the old problem of life and art, of experience and expression. Glad in the achievement of
the Young Men, he yet marveled how little of the true
brilliance of Solferino's had actually passed into print.
"Does a man's best," he mused, "ever get into his books?
I do not think so; and I say that with some knowledge
of men and literature and the certainty that, if I could
now meet Shakespeare, I should wonder why he had
declined upon such stuff as 'Hamlet' and 'Macbeth.' "[1]
Early in the 'nineties the Young Men thinking of their
chief may well have asked the same question and made
the same reply. To them Henley the talker was forever
stronger and more inspiring than Henley the writer. The
Views and Reviews were but fragments of his more
copious speech, brief glimpses into his larger critical
vision. And the *Book of Verses*, for all its fine sentiment
and finished technique, remained a mere shadow of the
richer poetic temperament. Yet Henley himself saw that
in the long run his whole personality would be judged
by that part of it which had found objective realization. Ultimately his accomplishment would count for
more than his intention; when Fellowship had deserted
him and he stood alone like Everyman at the tribunal,
Good Deeds, he knew, would prove his only advocate.
Throughout his criticism he was always conscious of "a
certain indestructible element of rightness" in Disraeli's
cynical contention that the critic was simply the man
who had "failed in literature and art."[2] He was therefore
always fearful lest his own critical work might be regarded as evidence of a creative failure. On looking
back over the period of his apprenticeship, he felt compelled to apologize for his assiduous addiction to journal-

[1] Henley, "Memoir," *Things Seen*, p. xxvii.
[2] See Henley, *Works*, iv, 363, n.

ism.[3] During his years at the helm of the *National Observer*, he could no longer content himself with the editing and appraising of other men's work; from the most crowded hours of his life, he reserved time to compose the mature poetry on which his own reputation as artist eventually would rest.

In 1892 David Nutt issued the second volume of Henley's lyrics as *The Song of the Sword and Other Verses*. To most readers, however, the title-poem represented little more than a sublimation of the Regatta's purposeful belligerency; while the unique significance of the volume arose from the suggestive "Rhymes and Rhythms" and the remarkable sequence called "London Voluntaries." Convinced that the whole book constituted "in some sort a manifesto," Arthur Symons described the "Voluntaries" as "the most individual, the most characteristically modern, and the most entirely successful of Mr. Henley's work in verse." Here at last, he said, was "a poet who [could] so enlarge the limits of his verse as to take in London"; and this alone "might be the test of poetry which professe[d] to be modern,— its capacity for dealing with London, with what one sees or might see there, indoors and out." The originality, of course, was patent; but there was also "something classical—a note of *Lycidas*—in these most modern of poems, as if modernity had become classical."[4] And "in certain fragments" the poet came "nearer than any other English singer to . . . the achievement of Verlaine and the ideal of the Decadence: to be a disembodied voice, and yet the voice of a human soul."[5] Henley had no interest in understanding the peculiar connotation Symons attached to the term "decadence"; and assuredly he had no desire that his name should be linked to that of the "absinthiated" Frenchman. But the

[3] See Preface, *Poems* (London, 1898), p. iii.

[4] Arthur Symons, "Mr. Henley's Poetry," *Fortnightly Review*, LVIII (1892), 183-84, 190.

[5] Symons, "The Decadent Movement in Literature," *Harper's New Monthly Magazine*, XXXVII (1893), 867.

comparison with Milton was flattering; and the eulogy in general was too warm to despise. It may, therefore, have been a mark of deference to the critic that in 1893 *The Song of the Sword* volume entered its second edition under the general title *London Voluntaries*.

The "modernity" of the "Voluntaries" lay less in the actual theme than in the poet's approach to his subject. Earlier artists in verse from Chaucer to Austin Dobson had written wisely and well of London characters and London stones, of revels at the Mermaid Tavern and oglings in St. James's Park. But no poet before Henley had viewed the city as other than an inanimate background for the multitudinous life it harbored[6]; none had concerned himself, like the Dickens of *Bleak House* and *Great Expectations*, with the actual personality of London, with the place-spirit that brooded over its wharves and warehouses, its cathedrals and courts of chancery. Comparable in effect to Baudelaire's impressionistic *Tableaux parisiens*, the "Voluntaries" first adapted English verse to the depiction of the metropolis as a great organism throbbing with its own vitality. Whereas previous London verse had served to tell the story of Londoners, Henley's poems forsook all narrative or satiric purpose in order to create an atmosphere.

In design the sequence approximates a symphonic structure; following a brief introduction entitled *Grave*, it develops its theme through four movements, *Andante con Moto, Scherzando, Largo e Mesto,* and *Allegro maëstoso.* As a composite whole, it captures the essence of London in its many moods. We hear the laughter of lovers by the River in the "sober Sabbath" twilight and the chime of "St. Margaret's bells, quiring their innocent

---

[6] In the beautiful sonnet, "Composed upon Westminster Bridge," Wordsworth indicates a feeling for the "mighty heart" of London; significantly, however, the heart "is lying still." Victorian poems before Henley, Buchanan's *London Poems* (1866), Locker's *London Lyrics* (1857, 1871), treat merely of the London background. Henley's influence is noticeable in later poems, such as Lawrence Binyon's *London Visions* (1895), which treat of the London spirit.

old world canticles." All night we ride through the
"avenues of sleep" "between their carcenets of linking
gold." At the "first sudden plash of dawn" we glimpse

> A rakehell cat—how furtive and acold!—
> A spent witch homing from some infamous dance.
> Obscene, quick-trotting, see her tip and fade
> Through shadowy railings into a pit of shade.

Then, our eyes wide with wonder, we behold the day
breaking in the east, some

> . . . miracle . . . happening in the air,
> Charging the very texture of the gray
> With something luminous and rare.

For the moment ours is the intense vision of the poet;
for the moment we sense as he the mysterious spell of
the hushed morning where even the

> . . . footfall craves
> Forgiveness of the majesty it braves.

Suddenly the tempo shifts to a gay *scherzo*; and we
enter a London transmuted by the yellow sunshine of an
October afternoon:

> 'Tis El Dorado—El Dorado plain,
> The Golden City! And when a girl goes by,
> Look! as she turns her glancing head,
> A call of gold is floated from her ear!
> Golden, all golden! In a golden glory,
> Long-lapsing down a golden coasted sky,
> The day, not dies but, seems
> Dispersed in wafts and drifts of gold, and shed
> Upon a past of golden song and story
> And memories of gold and golden dreams.

But the golden city pales as the fog, dank and terrible,
locks London in the death embrace:

> Out of the poisonous East,
> Over a continent of blight,
> Like a maleficent Influence released
> From the most squalid cellarage of hell,

The Wind-Fiend, the abominable—
The Hangman-Wind that tortures temper and light—
Comes slouching, sullen and obscene,
Hard on the skirts of the embittered night. . . .

The fear of the winter fog passes only with the spring
winds blowing "over leagues of myrtle blossoms and
may"; and once more "the lovely leafage of the Park
touch[es] to an ecstasy the act of seeing."

The unmistakable power of the "London Voluntaries" more than counterbalances the minor, if noticeable, defects. While the effort to crystallize within narrow compass a full experience of the city places an
occasional constraint upon the diction, the general movement of the poems harmonizes naturally with the moods
to be evoked. Throughout the sequence, the verse is
"free" in the best sense of the word; its form is dependent entirely upon the chosen tempo; rhyme falls not at
random, but wherever it may reinforce the meaning.
Despite grandiloquence of phrasing, the imagery attains an unusual honesty in depicting the "romance" of
living without evading the objective vision of "reality";
in the El Dorado of sunshine there remains the "blind
man pottering on the kerb"; and in the night-fog we
watch

. . . the poor, loitering harlot rather choose
Go pinched and pined to bed
Than lurk and shiver and curse her wretched way
From arch to arch, scouting some threepenny prey.

Through his acceptance of the sordid with the beautiful, the poet identifies himself empathically with his
subject; from within he times the pulse of the whole
city. And in so gauging a vast collective consciousness,
he approaches the later *"unanimisme"* of Jules Romains.
Majestically, *allegro maëstoso*, the last of the poems
records a mass reaction to the coming of spring; Pan,
"gay genius of a million Mays," stirs "the wills of man
and woman,"

187

To share his shameless, elemental mirth
In one great act of faith: while deep and strong,
Incomparably nerved and cheered,
The enormous heart of London joys to beat
To the measures of his rough majestic song;
The lewd, perennial, overmastering spell
That keeps the rolling universe ensphered,
And life, and all for which life lives to long,
Wanton and wondrous and for ever well.

Lines like these represent the mature poet's conquest of a morbid self-awareness. Himself attuned to the enormous beating heart of London, Henley submerges his own egotism in the ebb-and-flow of a universal life.

If the general arrangement of the "Voluntaries" follows a symphonic pattern, isolated descriptive passages —the visions of the sun-drenched square and the lamp-lit streets—derive from the technique of painting. This derivation appears even more clearly in several of the "Rhymes and Rhythms" where the design is pictorial rather than musical. In these poems Henley approaches nature with the graphic artist's feeling for line and color. As a result, his description of the trees, "midsummer-manifold, each one voluminous, a labyrinth of life," parallels exactly his prose description of Theodore Rousseau's forest scenes.[7] In effect his interpretation of

The shining, sensitive silver of the sea
Touched with the strange-hued blazonings of dawn

approximates the mood of Monet. And his depiction of thunderclouds recalls the night-pieces of Van Gogh[8]:

Space and dread and the dark—
Over a livid stretch of sky
Cloud-monsters crawling, like a funeral train
Of huge, primeval presences
Stooping beneath the weight
Of some enormous, rudimentary grief.

[7] *Cf. Works*, i, 147, and iv, 278.
[8] While Henley could scarcely have known of Van Gogh's work, he was without doubt familiar with the ideals of the post-impressionists.

Above all, his treatment of light and shade suggests the canvases of Whistler:

> The Sun, as he journeys
> His round on the lower
> Ascents of the blue,
> Washes the roofs
> And the hillsides with clarity;
> Charms the dark pools
> Till they break into pictures;
> Scatters magnificent
> Alms to the beggar trees;
> Touches the mist-folk,
> That crowd to his escort,
> Into translucencies
> Radiant and ravishing:
> As with the visible
> Spirit of Summer
> Gloriously vaporised,
> Visioned in gold!

One poem makes explicit his debt to the American master. The lines "To James McNeill Whistler" evoke the expected response to the Thames pictures:

> Under a stagnant sky,
> Gloom out of gloom uncoiling into gloom,
> The River, jaded and forlorn,
> Welters and wanders wearily—wretchedly—on;
> Yet in and out among the ribs
> Of the old skeleton bridge, as in the piles
> Of some dead lake-built city, full of skulls,
> Worm-worn, rat-riddled, mouldy with memories,
> Lingers to babble to a broken tune
> (Once, O, the unvoiced music of my heart!)
> So melancholy a soliloquy as it might tell
> The secret of the unending grief-in-grain,
> The terror of Time and Change and Death,
> That wastes this floating, transitory world.

To Mrs. Pennell these "verses . . . gave the very feeling, the magical charm of the Nocturnes."[9] And Whis-

---

[9] E. R. and J. Pennell, *The Life of James McNeill Whistler*, 2 vols. (Philadelphia, 1919), II, 97. *Cf.* T. R. Way and G. R. Dennis, *The Art of James McNeill Whistler* (London, 1905), p. 56.

tler apparently agreed; for he offered one of the "Nocturnes" as an illustration of the poem to be included in the *London Garland*.

In bringing to his poetry the techniques of music and painting, Henley appeared to be linking himself, in spite of himself, to the "decadent" group whose ideals he had consistently attacked. Not less than Wilde's "Symphony in Yellow" or Symonds's improvisation "In the Key of Blue," the "Rhymes and Rhythms" seemed to exemplify Baudelaire's theory of *les correspondances* as propounded in *Les Fleurs du mal*. But the influence of this theory on Henley's poetic style was more apparent than real. Whereas Symonds and Wilde established a correlation of the arts in an effort to develop verse entirely within an aesthetic dimension and thus entirely apart from an exterior reality, Henley drew upon various techniques in order to enlarge the scope of his poetry as a medium for the "expression of life." The aesthetes saw in the correspondence of word and sound and color a justification of art for art's sake; Henley found in it the means of attaining a higher poetic realism.

Though the structure of the descriptive poems among the "Rhymes and Rhythms" suggested a possible liaison with the literary "decadence," the content of the shorter lyrics made it clear that the poet had in no way compromised his lifelong activist ideals. One grim ballad raised the vigorous "masculine protest" against an effete romantic yearning for the hermaphrodite's asexuality.[10] Another heaped scorn upon the Fabian's dream of a purely rationalistic society across which the ancient gallows-tree would cast no shadow.[11] In general, the verses reflected a mature acceptance of the full experience, a willingness to face the eternal conflict of life and death. Inevitably, since the poems stemmed from the richest period of Henley's emotional development, life

[10] See "Rh. & Rh.," IX, *Works*, I, 131-32; and *cf.* Tennyson's "On One who affected an Effeminate Manner" (1889).
[11] See "Rh. & Rh.," XVII, *"Carmen Patibulare," Works*, I, 139-40.

seemed the greater reality. Life was the call to adventure, quickening man's desire "to strive, to seek, to find":

> From faded hopes and hopes agleam,
>> It calls you, calls you night and day
> Beyond the dark into the dream
>> Over the hills and far away.

Death, on the other hand, seemed remote and abstract.
Death was the distant symbol of completion, the re-
minder to man that regret for the past invalidated life
in the present, that the Conqueror Worm would one
day mock the doubter:

> "Poor fool that might—
> That might, yet would not, dared not, let this be,
> Think of it, here and thus made over to me
> In the implacable night!"

But death in itself could be no evil. Even in the years
of high resolve and full accomplishment, death remained
to Henley an intellectual necessity. Quietly, almost dispassionately, he could watch the infant Margaret laps-
ing from Anna's hands into "some comforting corner of
sleep"; and calmly he could meditate upon her rest:

> So you wake in your bed,
> Having lived, having loved;
> But the shadows are there,
> And the world and its kingdoms
> Incredibly faded;
> And you grope through the Terror
> Above you and under
> For the light, for the warmth,
> The assurance of life;
> But the blasts are ice-born,
> And your heart is nigh burst
> With the weight of the gloom
> And the stress of your strangled
> And desperate endeavour:
> Sudden a hand—
> Mother, O Mother!—
> God at His best to you,

191

Out of the roaring,
Impossible silences,
Falls on and urges you,
Mightily, tenderly,
Forth, as you clutch at it,
Forth to the infinite
Peace of the Grave.[12]

This was one of the few subjective lyrics in Henley's second volume and one that would acquire a new and tragic significance when the world and its kingdoms, the insubstantial pageant of London, had faded beyond recall.

[12] This poem is dated "October 1891"; in the 1898 volume and in the *Works*, it is dedicated to the memory of Margaret Emma Henley.

⧌ CHAPTER 13. "THE WRACKFUL SIEGE." THE PERSONAL TRAGEDY: 1894-1898

THE publication of the *London Voluntaries* placed Henley beyond question in the first rank of late-Victorian lyrists. Ten years earlier when writing to Austin Dobson in praise of the *Old World Idylls*, he remarked wistfully that he "should have liked to be a poet, too."[1] Now no longer was he obliged to speak of his ambition in the conditional past tense. His reputation as poet spread in widening circles beyond the literary coteries of London. Readers who had escaped his personal influence and who knew nothing of the warfaring Regatta or the brilliant *Observer* found a freshness and vigor in his regular and free verses. From America came the earnest salute of a young man, weary of the decorous Taylor and the mellifluous Gilder:

> Henley, a hand to thee across the seas!
> There's somewhat in thy rugged Saxon verse
> To fat the blood like lusty bullock's meat:
> And in thy May-day flutings 'neath the trees
> There's magic 'gainst the universal curse,—
> A healing balm as of thy meadows sweet.[2]

Appropriately enough, Scotland, which had first given Henley the opportunity of self-assertion, first made official recognition of his achievement. In 1893, shortly after the appearance of the *Voluntaries*, St. Andrews University conferred upon him the Doctor-of-Laws degree. More than any other tribute, this honor marked the high point of his career; it formally related him to the academic world from which by poverty and disease he had long since been excluded.

Henley's literary success had meaning to him only in the light of a more personal satisfaction. His true sense

[1] See Alban Dobson, *Austin Dobson*, p. 118.
[2] Edward Bright, Jr., "To W. E. H.," *Critic* (New York), XXVI (1895), 66.

of fulfillment arose from his faith that his own life had found its perpetuity in the consciousness of his child:

> O, leaf out of leaf is the way of the land,
> Wave out of wave of the sea,
> And who shall reckon what lives may live
> In the life that we bade to be?

But with the death of Margaret his struggle lost its purpose; his attainment became a vanity. On the eleventh of February, 1894, "Wendy" slipped into her last sleep; and Gilbert Parker from Mexico City sent a tender elegy "To the Emperor, Dead":

> My dear, I was thy lover.
> A man of spring-time years,
> I sang thee songs,—gave gifts and songs most poor,
> But they were signs: and now for evermore
> Thou farest forth! My heart is full of tears,
> My dear, my dear![3]

Yet the father himself wrote no poem to mark her passing. Silently he closed the house at Addiscombe and with Anna set out at once for Paris.[4] The failure of the *National Observer* six weeks later seemed a matter of small importance.[5]

During the summer following Margaret's death, Henley, half-mad with grief, moved to a gloomy cottage overlooking the river at Barnes. There one wet October evening Joseph Pennell and A. S. Hartrick found him "at his desk, . . a Viking Lear, . . cursing the weather and the place, explaining in an extraordinarily tragic manner how the tide in the river outside was taking his life away bit by bit every day, so that he had to shutter the windows to be safe."[6] When the visitors presented him with the drawings they had selected for his an-

---

[3] Gilbert Parker, *Critic* (New York), xxi (1894), 206.

[4] See Pennell, *Joseph Pennell*, i, 272.

[5] The *National Observer* continued under new management with Frank Harris as editor. Harris announced Henley's resignation, April 7, 1894; see *NO*, xi, 515.

[6] Hartrick, quoted by Pennell from a letter, *Joseph Pennell*, i, 297-98.

MARGARET E. HENLEY (1895)
By the Marchioness of Granby

thology of London verse, he bellowed his disapproval
with such unnatural vehemence that Hartrick suspected
mental derangement. Suddenly Anna burst into the
room, laughing, laughing at her husband's oaths, laughing him into a realization of his folly. Straightway he
subsided, apologized for his erratic behavior, re-exam-
ined the drawings, and "passed" them with his blessing.
This incident was an index both of his despair and of
his one hope for recovery. The courage and sympathy
of the Châtelaine alone could revive in him a belief in
the purpose of living. Before the end of the year he had
accepted the editorship of William Heinemann's *New
Review*.[7]

Early in December, when Henley was aligning contributions to the first issue of his monthly, a report
reached him of Stevenson's death at Vailima. Immedi-
ately he commissioned William Archer to prepare an
obituary which might be included in the January number. On reconsidering the report, however, he decided
that it could be nothing more than an unfounded rumor;
and he wrote to Archer that he had withdrawn the
obituary in the firm belief that the news was merely "a
daring and devilish plant." If it were true, the notice, of
course, would not be lost; and if it were not, Archer,
like all of "Lewis's" old friends, would rejoice and be
exceeding glad. . . . But within a few days delayed
telegrams from San Francisco had made doubt no longer
possible. Before long Henley was compelled to write a
second, and far more pathetic, letter, begging Archer
to bear with his indecision. He was loath to think of
Stevenson as dead before the wrong that had estranged
them could "be made right"; "And now," he said, "that's
impossible; and there is nothing for us but, as I wrote
of and to him langsyne, for us to

[7] Henley replaced Archibald Grove as editor, and J. W. Gilmer replaced Arthur Waugh as sub-editor; see Gosse's letter to Heinemann
concerning Henley and Waugh (Evan Charteris, ed., *Life and Letters
of Sir Edmund Gosse* [London, 1931], p. 235).

'Lie in the Peace of the Great Release
As once in the grass together.' "[8]

. . . So passed Louis, alienated beyond reconciliation,[9] the Shorter Catechist perhaps, but once the boon companion, the valiant in velvet, the only man who ever had understood the true nature of Henley's struggle. Archer's obituary to him duly appeared in the January number without editorial comment.

In the quality of its contributions the *New Review* was hardly less remarkable than the *National Observer*. As its first serial, it carried a brilliant fantasy entitled *The Time Machine*, which discovered to the public the latest of Henley's protégés, an unknown writer of amazing ingenuity.[10] In later issues Henry James traced through many pages and with extreme subtlety and exquisite indirection all that the precocious Maisie knew. C. B. Fry wrote with authority of cricket; while Wilfrid Blunt displayed a knowledge *recherché* of Arabian horses. Sir Charles Dilke pled for a strengthening of Her Majesty's Navy; and Frederick Greenwood warned England of imminent European alliances. Critically— Alice Meynell measured the achievement of Christina Rossetti; George Steevens analyzed the art of Ibsen; and T. E. Brown re-interpreted the major Elizabethans. Lyrically—Verlaine and Kipling, Katharine Tynan and Stephen Phillips represented conflicting strains in the new poetry. Names so distinguished ensured an imposing monthly roster. But where, we ask, across this brilliance shone "the trail of Henley?" For the distinctive

[8] Quoted by Charles Archer, *William Archer*, pp. 214-15.

[9] The real denouement of the quarrel came with the criticism of the *Weir of Hermiston* manuscript in November, 1895. On reading the fragment, Henley wrote to Colvin that he had found his "Lewis" again, "and in all his glory, in this the last work of his hand."— Quoted by Lucas, *The Colvins*, p. 244.

[10] At Henley's request H. G. Wells expanded several short stories, previously published anonymously in the *National Observer*. Wells dedicated the finished novel to Henley. See Geoffrey West, *H. G. Wells* (London, 1930), p. 102. Wilde wrote from Reading Gaol asking news of Henley's protégé; see *De Profundis* (New York, 1926), p. 17.

note, the unifying force, behind the *Observer*, we look in vain. Among the regular contributors, to be sure, there remained several members of the old Regatta, Wyndham, Whibley, Gilbert Parker, Marriott-Watson; but in a periodical where there was no place for anonymous reviewing and no room for unsigned squibs in verse and prose, there could be no real occasion for the omnipresent Henleyan epigrams or the flashing paradoxes of the Young Men. If obvious at all, the editor's influence may be detected only in his choice of matter for publication. Walter Raleigh thought it was "very good of Henley who want[ed] crackle and flash" to include his article on Sir John Harington, written, as it was, in "the approved Dict. Nat. Biog. [*sic*] style."[11] And Joseph Conrad was sufficiently reassured by Henley's acceptance of *The Nigger of the Narcissus*, his first successful novel, to persevere in the writing of fiction.[12] Encouragement so well placed would alone have imparted to the editorship an unusual significance.

Though Henley wrote little criticism or poetry during the years of the *New Review*, he found other literary pursuits to absorb his leisure time. With Charles Whibley he collaborated in 1895 on the *Book of English Prose*, an anthology designed to complement the *Lyra Heroica* which had appeared four years earlier. With George Wyndham he prepared an edition of Wilfrid Blunt's poems. And with John S. Farmer he began the compilation of *Slang and Its Analogues*, a dictionary in seven volumes which eventually would serve as the standard authority on vulgar usage. Unassisted he selected a *London Garland* "from five centuries of English verse," and a book of *English Lyrics* "from Chaucer to Poe." Several of his editorial projects failed to materialize. His issue of Byron's letters, for instance, had

11 Raleigh, *Letters*, I, 189.
12 See Joseph Conrad, "Introduction," Thomas Beer, *Stephen Crane* (New York, 1923), p. 4. It is interesting to note that the *New Review* also published Stephen Crane's "Horses."

not passed beyond the first volume when it was anticipated by the less inspired footnoting of R. E. Prothero;
and his series of *English Classics* was abandoned for
reasons unknown soon after the publication of *The
Lives of the Poets.* As the most ambitious of his many
editions, the *Tudor Translations* raised the largest single
monument to his good taste and sound scholarship.
Scorning the ornate typography which Morris and
Ricketts thought beautiful, Henley arranged with Walter Blaikie and David Nutt that the *Translations* should
be printed on fine paper and bound with severe elegance
in plain gray covers.[13] Though he himself contributed
none of the introductions, he commissioned able critics
to furnish prefatory essays; and these he subjected to
complete revision. Finally completed by Whibley, the
series made accessible in attractive form some of the
liveliest pages in English writing.[14] And in so doing it
provided a model for composition, calculated, like the
epigrammatic style of the Regatta, to counteract the
languid prose of the "decadents."[15]

But whatever the success of his literary ventures during the management of the *New Review*, Henley was
unable to regain the peace of mind, the fullness of assent, that had made the direction of the *National Observer* the great experience of his career. After the
deaths of Margaret and Louis, two major reverses in
public life conspired to enhance his private griefs. In
July, 1895, Arthur Waugh wrote, in his "London Letter"
to the New York *Critic*, that there seemed to be "very
little doubt" that Mr. Henley would "be appointed to
the chair of English Literature at Edinburgh. . . . The

[13] For a discussion of Henley's interest in typography, see Elizabeth
Robins Pennell, "William Ernest Henley, Lover of the Art of Book-
making," *Colophon*, Part V, Section 9, pp. 1-12.

[14] Professor F. O. Matthiessen pays tribute to the editorial work of
Henley and Whibley; see Matthiessen, *Translation: An Elizabethan
Art* (Cambridge, Mass., 1931), p. viii.

[15] Compton Mackenzie points to the *Translations* as the most effective counterdecadent publications; see Mackenzie, *Literature in My
Time* (New York, 1933), p. 129.

post would only necessitate half a year's sojourn in the Scots capital, so that it would practically have little effect upon Mr. Henley's literary occupations in the South." Though the list of rival candidates included William Sharp, Walter Raleigh, George Saintsbury, Churton Collins, and Eric Robinson, Henley was encouraged by London friends to regard all claims as less considerable than his own.[16] He was therefore sadly disappointed in August when Lord Balfour of Burleigh announced that the post had gone to Saintsbury. Wyndham was scarcely surprised by the Government's choice, insofar as he felt that Henley belonged "to that peculiar order, so trying to their friends, who are obviously excellent and yet, apparently, incapable of getting anything."[17] Henley, however, drew comfort from his belief that the Prime Minister was reserving for him the office of Poet Laureate to be awarded in November. But here, too, his hope was dashed; and his dejection was merely intensified by the fact that the honor had been granted "such an ape as Alfred Austin."[18] The effect of these disappointments should not be exaggerated; yet it cannot wholly be ignored. A sense of defeat brooded over Henley's last days in London, a feeling of exhaustion and spent passion; and there was an unmistakably tragic overtone to his selection of a motto for his late poems:

O, how shall summer's honey breath hold out
Against the wrackful siege of battering days?

Early in 1898, the *New Review* joined its predecessors in limbo; and the editor, an old man before his time, found himself cut off from any permanent source of income. At the crucial moment A. J. Balfour procured for him a pension sufficiently large to preserve him from complete indigence.[19] Henley then retired from the

16 See Raleigh, *Letters*, I, 186.
17 Quoted by Mackail and Wyndham, *George Wyndham*, I, 288.
18 See Kennedy Williamson, *W. E. Henley* (London, 1930), p. 229.
19 See Cornford, *Henley*, p. 59. The pension brought Henley an annual income of two hundred and twenty-five pounds.

tumult of Fleet Street to the privacy of a transformed tavern at Muswell Hill. There he prepared a collected edition of his poems and continued his work on the *Tudor Translations*. There also he wrote his *London Types*,[20] an ironic last commentary on life in the City, of which one reviewer wrote: "These are capital photographs, which may be interesting a hundred years hence; but they are not pretty, and we are loth to call them art."[21] The judgment may well have amused the poet, and, at the same time, led him to wonder just how deep had been the influence of his own criticism, which manfully had striven to dispel the confusion between art and prettiness. But a few there were who never questioned his importance. To the Regatta he remained the master till the end; when editing Shakespeare's sonnets, Wyndham wrote to Whibley concerning the health of "*our* Will."[22] Francis Thompson who had never known him in his prime thought of him in age as a becalmed Olympian; and when he visited Muswell Hill with Lewis Hind, he "quite naturally took a stool at his feet, while Henley a splendid leonine figure, hair and beard now white, lounged in a high chair."[23] In the summer of 1898 Teddy came from New York; a mere youth still, he seemed, bursting with news of his latest roles and romances, urging William to spend the winter at Lake Placid where together they might operate a private theater. But by mid-October Teddy had become one with the dead actors of his brother's ballade. Henley mourned his passing; yet he could not rebuke the fates that had willed it. For he had learned to accept many things; and even death had lost its horror.

[20] This was a series of thirteen "quatorzains," designed for illustration by William Nicholson, published 1898.

[21] *Athenaeum*, 1901[2], p. 838, unsigned review.

[22] Quoted by Mackail and Wyndham, *George Wyndham*, I, 337.

[23] C. Lewis Hind, "W. E. Henley," *Authors and I* (New York, 1921), p. 131.

⧫§ CHAPTER 14. "SOME LATE LARK SINGING."
LAST POEMS: 1889-1903

PAUL KRUGER's ultimatum to the British agent at Pretoria set at defiance the "frantic boast" of the Jubilee orators. And long months of disastrous war tried a theoretical imperialism in a practical ordeal by fire. From retirement Henley saw falling on distant battlefields the political ideals for which he had campaigned and the bravest of the Young Men with whom he had made the *Observer* belligerent. Hysterically he wrote his songs *For England's Sake* in an effort to persuade himself and his countrymen of England's invincibility. But his enthusiasm rang hollow; and his true helplessness was of a piece with the desperate joy of London on Mafeking Day. Yet, whatever its poetic value, his doggerel indicated an awareness of the forces that were terminating an era of great endeavor and remarkable achievement. At its worst it was a far more vital utterance than the last pathetic cry of Wilde. It was designed to enspirit a bewildered but living nation; while the confessions of the vagrant Sebastian Melmoth served merely as epilogue to a dead "decadence."

The verses *For England's Sake* had then a significance in the fact that they revealed a late Henley still prepared to face the actuality of pain. The greater and more typical poetry of these last years represented the realist's final attempt to fit the exigencies of his time into a larger pattern. At Worthing on the Channel coast, where he now moved his home, Henley learned with consternation of the reverses in Africa. But above the din of battle, he heard the high-sounding sea; and he asked the meaning of its ceaseless ebb-and-flow. He saw the evil of society; and yet he believed in the incorruptibility of "the wonderful world." In moments of despair he wrote ballads of marching men. In long hours of calm he made lyrics of the natural procession, of the endless, measured cycle of birth and death and rebirth.

Henley's final testament of beauty, *Hawthorn and Lavender*, is a sequence of fifty last "echoes," relating man's life to the pageant of the changing seasons. The grandiose *"Praeludium"* to the tempo *Largo expressivo* elegizes the dead year and prophesies the new life:

> . . . On the spirit of Man
> And on the heart of the World there falls
> A strange, half-desperate peace:
> A war-worn, militant, gray jubilance
> In the unkind, implacable tyranny
> Of Winter, the obscene,
> Old, crapulous Regent, who in his loins—
> O, who but feels he carries in his loins
> The wild, sweet-blooded, wonderful harlot,
> Spring?

Across the dolorous February night, through "a dream that warms like wine" rings the faraway chime of hope. And athwart the evil gales of March comes the courageous call of the "fierce, protesting lark." Soon the sea-wind stirs to life the ice-bound spirit:

> Sound, Sea of England, sound and shine,
> Blow, English Wind, amain,
> Till in this old, gray heart of mine
> The Spring need wake again!

With the birth of Spring the blackbird tunes once more his boxwood flute:

> Caught with us all in the nets of fate,
> So the sweet wretch sings early and late;
> And, O my fairest, after all,
> The heart of the World's in his innocent call.
> The will of the World's with him wing and wing:—
> "Life—life—life! 'Tis the sole great thing
> This side of death,
> Heart on heart in the wonder of Spring!"
> So the bird saith—
> The wise bird saith!

Life heeds his song and arises, new-souled in "the insolent, high-blooded May," resolved to fulfill itself before its time is spent. And when the May has vanished, only the love-token, the subtle wreath of hair, will stay to tell of youth in springtide:

> Poor souls—they have but time and place
> To play their transient little play
> And sing their singular little song,
> Ere they are rushed away
> Into the antient, undisclosing Night;
> And none is left to tell of the clear eyes
> That filled them with God's grace,
> And turned the iron skies to skies of gold!
> None; but the sweetest She herself grows old—
> Grows old, and dies;
> And, but for such a lovely snatch of hair
> As this, none—none could guess, or know
> That She was kind and fair,
> And he had nights and days beyond compare—
> How many dusty and silent years ago!

"The green, delicious plenitude of June" itself forebodes the passing of the Summer, "stately and splendid," "sad with satiety," "sick with fulfilment." Before long, October's harvest brings a brief regret for what might have been. And November, stripping forest and garden, dims the memory of June:

> These were the woods of wonder
> We found so close and boon
> When the bride-month in her beauty
> Lay mouth to mouth with June.
>
> November, the old, lean widow
> Sniffs, and snivels, and shrills,
> And the bowers are all dismantled,
> And the long grass wets and chills.[1]

Thus the year approaches its close; and the poet who

[1] These lines are remarkably similar, in manner and matter, to the shorter lyrics of Heine; cf. above, pp. 92-93.

203

has played his role prepares to withdraw from the scene before the pageant is renewed:

> So let me hence as one
> Whose part in the world has been dreamed out and done:
> One that hath fairly earned and spent
> In pride of heart and jubilance of blood
> Such wages, be they counted bad or good,
> As Time, the old taskmaster, was moved to pay. . . .

Fully developed in *Hawthorn and Lavender*, the parallel between man's life and the cycle of the seasons had, long before Henley's volume, worn thin as a poetic *leitmotif*. Generations of earlier lyrists had made facile rhymes associating a young man's wayward fancy with the merry month of May and an old man's boding of death with the bleak December. Thus, however vital may have been Henley's experience of April rain and June roses, his natural imagery frequently lapses into triteness and so fails to evoke a fresh response to the phenomenal world. Yet the true power of *Hawthorn and Lavender* remains independent of its value as nature poetry. In effect the whole sequence stands as a single love lyric to Anna; nature provides a framework, but faith through time is the actual theme. The moon is less a heavenly body than a symbol of the enduring forces beyond and above life; man is fated

> Soon, all-too-soon,
> Ungainly and forlorn to lie
> Full in the eye
> Of the cynical, discomfortable moon
> That, as I looked, stared from the fading sky,
> A clown's face flour'd for work.[2]

But love, transcending time, outmocks the cosmic irony; and the lover feels intimations of a pre-existence, as old as time itself:

[2] Henley's imagery here anticipates Carl Sandburg's "imagist" poem, "Night Stuff."

When, in what other life,
Where in what old, spent star,
Systems ago, dead vastitudes afar,
Were we two bird and bough, or man and wife?
Or wave and spar?

And love carries over into the future, till even the grave
foregoes its "obscene victory":

Come by my bed,
What time the gray ghost shrieks and flies;
Take in your hands my head,
And look, O look, into my failing eyes;
And by God's grace,
Even as He sunders body and breath,
The shadow of your face
Shall pass with me into the run
Of the Beyond, and I shall keep and save
Your beauty, as it used to be,
An absolute part of me,
Lying there, dead and done,
Far from the sovran bounty of the sun,
Down in the grisly colonies of the Grave.

In these verses, passion is lifted above sentimentality by
the sheer strength of the poet's emotion. "Come by my
bed," in its mellowness, directness, and sincerity, is the
work of an "unconceited" Donne concerned with the
ultimate issue of mortality.

Shortly after the appearance of *Hawthorn and Lavender* in book-form,[3] Henley moved his home from
Worthing to Woking in Surrey whence he might more
easily "commute" to London. There he prepared his
complete edition of Fielding and continued to sort cards
innumerable for the great slang dictionary. In his garden
at the edge of a pinewood he received old friends and
new admirers. Among the latter, Alfred Harmsworth,

[3] *HL* first appeared in the *North American Review*, CLXIX (1899),
593-603; CLXXII (1901), 895-905; CLXXIII (1901), 418-21. David
Nutt published the volume in 1901.

Lord Northcliffe, who was finding it increasingly profitable to avoid Henley's journalistic indiscretions, called frequently to discuss the state of the nation and the affairs of the empire. One memorable afternoon early in the spring of 1903, Northcliffe invited the poet to accompany him on a motor-drive in his proud new Mercédes, a "shapeless, unhandsome" vehicle, yet one strong with "the strength of some seventy-five horses." As if for the first time, Henley saw the rolling countryside, its "beauties and privacies," the sea and the heath, all as one endless panorama. With breathless reverence, he chronicled the novel experience in his last poem, the triumphing *Song of Speed*:

> Where the Stars in the Morning
> Go singing together
> For joy in the dazzling,
> Naked, unvisited
> Emperies of Space!
> And the heart in your breast
> Sings, as the World
> Slips past like a dream
> Of Speed.

With Speed came the primordial summons to life, life snatched from "the black, irresistible legions of Death,"

> For the antient, invincible
> Spirit of Man,
> Stern-set, adventurous,
> Dreaming things, doing things. . . .

The automobile was but the latest of gifts to a mankind struggling briefly against an eternity of time; it was a miracle wrested from the grasp of a God who gloried in man's creative activity,

> Smiling as Whistler,
> Smiling as Kelvin,
> And Rodin and Tolstoi,
> And Lister and Strauss

206

> (That with his microbes,
> This with his fiddles!),
> Tugged at His fingers
> And worked out His meanings.

The Mercédes epitomized the toil of a productive century, the labor of

> Mind after mind,
> On fire with discovery,
> Filled full with the fruits
> Of an hundred fat years,
> And mad with the dreams
> And desires of To-Day.

In Speed lay "the new scheme" of living. And the activist at the end of his own span welcomed the innovation.

The *Song of Speed* stood as Henley's final synthesis of the elements that had made his life meaningful. Lister's skill, Whistler's craftsmanship, Rodin's creative genius, Tolstoi's heroic acceptance, these had given direction and inspiration to his personal struggle. In the manifold achievement of his time he saw a last resolution of the conflict between fate and free will. The clutch of circumstance remained an inescapable reality; but the unconquerable soul asserting its intrinsic divinity found fulfillment within the laws preordained for its existence. Utilizing matter as the essential medium of expression, the scientist, no less than the artist, "worked out" the patterns of a universal design. The machine, like the picture or the sonata, contributed to the enrichment of human experience; and only the maladjusted romantic could deny its purpose.

From his arrival in the August mist at the Royal Edinburgh Infirmary to his first enraptured acquaintance with the "amazing Mercédes," Henley had been forever conscious of the drama in living. And it was by a singular stroke of dramatic irony that he was precipitated towards his death. Scarcely had he published his *Song of Speed*, glorying in man's mechanical invention, when

207

he suffered fatal injury in dismounting from a moving railway carriage. His fall awakened in his system the long-dormant tubercular germ; and in his last weeks at Woking he endured greater physical pain than he had known at any time since his agonized vigil in hospital. But on the eleventh of July, a few hours before the end, he regained a brief, untroubled composure. With Anna standing by his bed, he died in peace.

৵ঌ CHAPTER 15. EPILOGUE. ST. PAUL'S:
JULY 11, 1907

IN THE Crypt of St. Paul's, on the fourth anniversary of Henley's death, Lord Plymouth unveiled a bronze replica of the bust sculptured by Rodin some twenty years earlier. Austin Dobson, Frederick Greenwood, Thomas Hardy, George Saintsbury, G. S. Street, H. G. Wells, teachers, admirers, disciples, these had come to honor the poet's memory. Plymouth read the warm tribute of George Meredith who was himself unable to attend the ceremony; Henley, he said, "was one of the main supports of good literature in our time," a man whose "inspiriting heartiness and inciting counsels gathered about him a troop of young writers who are proud in acknowledging their debt to him."[1] George Wyndham then delivered an *éloge* which Rodin had written from Paris; and to this he added a personal appreciation of his master's work. The service concluded with a benediction pronounced by the Archdeacon of London.

Late in the autumn of 1910 Wyndham made plans for a reunion of "five or six or seven who belonged to W. E. H.,"[2] a final gathering of all who were left of the worshipful Regatta. Henley's best "lines," he told Whibley, were fast "becoming parts of English speech"; the world at last had accepted a poet who once could find no publisher; and it was very fitting that the Young Men, no longer young, should exchange recollections of a great man whom the common reader had never known. Wyndham's respect for the Chief's character may possibly have led him to overestimate the poet's capacity for survival. Assuredly with the coming of the "modernists," Henley's name suffered total eclipse; and no bronze memorial could preserve the luster of his reputation. In

---

[1] Meredith, *Letters*, II, 600; see also "Memorial to W. E. Henley," *The Times*, July 12, 1907, p. 8.

[2] Wyndham, quoted by Mackail and Wyndham, *George Wyndham*, II, 677.

1922, Arthur Symons, revising his eulogy of 1892, questioned Henley's claim to remembrance; it would, he maintained, be a grave error to seek the origins of the new *vers libre* in the unrhymed Hospital poems or the cadenced "Rhymes and Rhythms," with which most of the "new poets" were wholly unfamiliar.[3] And the "new poets," for their part, felt no urge to re-interpret a minor lyrist of the "decadent" 'nineties, whom Alfred Noyes was imitating and attempting to revive,[4] and about whom the unhappy Vachel Lindsay was lecturing to boys' clubs.[5]

Ultimately, however, Wyndham's enthusiasm may prove more cogent than Symons's reconsidered appraisal. For Victorian reputations are no longer dependent upon the facile neo-Georgian dismissal of Victorian art. Already, to a world which has moved beyond the brittle intellection of the disillusioned 'twenties, the abundant humanity of Dickens seems less remote than the labyrinthine aestheticism of James Joyce. It is now a matter of small importance that Henley could not have influenced the "rhythmic dissonances" of the Sitwell clan. It remains of permanent significance that Henley beyond measure impressed and stimulated Yeats and Kipling, Wells and Conrad. In no complete revaluation of the 'nineties can the Viking chief and his Regatta be denied a major place. When the late Victorian period is viewed in its true perspective, the historian may, not inconceivably, point to Henley as an unreported nineteenth century Dr. Johnson. And indeed the resemblances between the critics are worthy of passing consideration. Sons of provincial booksellers, both fought poverty and disease to achieve pre-eminence in the literary life of London. Each, thwarted in his effort to obtain an Oxford degree, subsequently won, by sheer

[3] See Arthur Symons, "The Revival of Henley," *London Quarterly Review*, cxxxvii (1922), 16-22.

[4] Noyes echoes Henley in his imperial propaganda, in his seasonal poems, and in his London verse.

[5] See H. W. Wells, *New Poets and Old* (New York, 1940), p. 314.

force of self-acquired erudition, his doctorate from a British university outside England. Each, having failed as a dramatist, succeeded despite financial reverses as a journalist. Each turned his hand to lexicography; and each spent much time and energy upon admirable editions of the English classics. Each championed the political ideals of a Tory tradition; and each accepted a pension from a Tory government. Eventually each was honored by a memorial in St. Paul's Cathedral. These, to be sure, may be no more than accidental analogies. Yet beyond these remains an essential affinity of character and outlook. Both men cultivated a brusqueness of manner, in order to conceal a fundamental generosity of spirit; both were amiable poseurs. Philosophically, both sought to confute nebulous metaphysics with practical commonsense; both were "realists." Nevertheless, whatever parallels might be drawn between their compelling personalities, no one could seriously suggest that Henley would ever challenge Johnson's place as the "great Cham of literature." To the most respectful of the Young Men, Henley's critical work, for all its prophetic insight, could scarcely have seemed comparable, either in power or coherence, to Johnson's magnificent apology for a dying neo-classicism. Moreover, while the Regatta may well have deemed the verbal bouts at Solferino's as lively and brilliant as the best recorded conversations of the Literary Club, the unbiased historian could hardly place the isolated epigrams that have crept into memoir books over against the inexhaustible flow of wit and wisdom that the master-biographer has treasured up on purpose to a life beyond life.

Though his personality once far overshadowed his work, Henley the man, lacking a Boswell, can now be known only through his poetry. If few of his lyrics match the ecstasy of Francis Thompson or the metrical finish of A. E. Housman, his verse as a whole, read in the order of its composition, yet forms a record of self-

211

revelation entirely unique in the age of "decadence." From a fear of disease and a longing for release the poet moves toward a more and more strident assertion of the "will to live"; the sentimental reverie of the early Swinburnean stanzas yields to the grim, Heinesque "realism" with which *In Hospital* clings to the sensuous life, and this in turn gives way to the defiance of "*Invictus.*" Style then becomes the refuge for the ego that has escaped defeatism; and the difficult French forms of *Bric-à-brac* furnish the technical control necessary to a dispassionate portrayal of reality. Once capable of objective craftsmanship, the artist is prepared to accept his world and to communicate his vision of it with neither bitterness nor undue optimism; the "London Voluntaries" and the "Rhymes and Rhythms" render in words the response to living of the painter and the composer. Finally, his brief life's work completed, the poet looks steadily and soberly at death, no longer the archenemy but the inevitable solution; *Hawthorn and Lavender* attains a genuine depth through its concern with the last issue of man's experience. Naturally this spiritual evolution is not always in a straight line; lending a human vitality to Henley's work, there are countless unresolved conflicts, contradictions, recessions. But these are only aberrations; behind them all is the slow, unmistakable mellowing, the gradual arrival at a mature philosophy of life.

For all its variation of mood and manner, Henley's verse as a whole is dominated by a single persistent *leitmotif*, a "master quality," which leaves its indelible impression on the mind of the reader. No poet sings with greater authenticity of accent the worth of "the wonderful world"; and none communicates with greater insistency the haunting sense of time and change, the sense of "the dredful joye, alwey that slit so yerne." If his verse reduces a philosophy to its lowest common denominator, it yet reflects the great and universal sympathy, the power of acceptance, that endeared him

to the admiring Young Men. In it is mirrored an abundant faith in the mission of humanity, towards which the
"decadent" aesthetes could not aspire. But of its very
texture is a belief in the individual unconquerable soul,
a belief far beyond the comprehension of the totalitarian
artist. Many of the lyrics no more than half-articulate
this creed. But not a few utter its principles with a conviction and a finality which bring us close to the heart
of the man who wrote them. The best of Henley remains a sufficient proof that the devotion of the Regatta
was not misplaced.

INSOFAR as most of Henley's unsigned hack-work lies buried in the files of defunct periodicals, the following bibliography must be regarded as suggestive rather than exhaustive. Part I is designed to include the first and important later editions of Henley's published books, the titles and dates of his editorial projects, a representative group of his uncollected periodical articles, and a more or less complete check-list of critical and biographical studies casting direct light upon his life and work. Part II consists of a selection from the writings by and about Henley's contemporaries, in which we obtain the clearest picture of the Viking chief and his distinguished Regatta. Part III gathers together a few of the secondary works which have illuminated the literary, social, and historical backgrounds of Henley's career.

Unless otherwise indicated, the place of publication for all books is London.

PART I

THE WRITINGS OF WILLIAM ERNEST HENLEY

WORKS

The Works of W. E. Henley, 7 vols. 1908.
The Works of William Ernest Henley, 5 vols., including *Lyra Heroica*. 1921.

POEMS

"Hospital Sketches," *Cornhill Magazine*, XXXII (1875), 120-28.
"Hospital Sketches," H. B. Donkin, ed., *Voluntaries for an East London Hospital*. 1887.
Gleeson White, ed., *Ballades and Rondeaus, passim*. 1887.
A Book of Verses. 1888.
The Song of the Sword and Other Verses. 1892. Reissued as *London Voluntaries and Other Verses*. 1893.

London Types, quatorzains, illustrated by William Nicholson. New York, 1898.
Poems, with preface. 1898.
For England's Sake. 1900.
"Hawthorn and Lavender: Songs and Madrigals," *North American Review*, CLXIX (1899), 593-603, CLXXII (1901), 895-905, CLXXIII (1901), 418-21.
Hawthorn and Lavender. 1901.
A Song of Speed. 1903.

CRITICISM

"Chénier," *Encyclopaedia Britannica*, 9th edition, v, 581.
Thomas H. Ward, ed., *The English Poets*, 4 vols. 1880. Contains notes by Henley: "Robert Henryson," I, 137-39; "Samuel Butler," II, 396-99; "John Byrom," III, 230-32; "Charles Kingsley," IV, 608-9.
"London Letter," *Critic* (New York), at intervals, Feb. 27, 1886—Feb. 4, 1888; see *Critic*, XI (1889), 183.
Views and Reviews: Literature. 1890.
"The Tory Press and the Tory Party," *National Review*, XXI (1893), 268-71.
Henley and T. F. Henderson, "The Cult of Mary Campbell," *New Review*, XVI (1897), 674-86.
Views and Reviews: Art. 1901-1902.
Pall Mall Magazine articles: "The Hundred Best Novels," XVIII (1899), 422-26; "Some Notes on Charles Dickens," XVIII, 573-79; "Shakespeare in France," XIX (1899), 132-37; "Pippin," XIX, 278-83; "Balzac As He Was," XIX, 423-27; "Titbits Tyrannus," XIX, 581-86; "The Two Hugos," XX (1900), 134-38; "A Chapter on Dandies," XX, 279-83; "Memories," XX, 423-27; "In Cap and Bells," XX, 566-71; "In Milton's Hand," XXI (1900), 135-39; "Concerning Atkins," XXI, 280-83; "*I. M. R. A. M. S.*," XXI, 423-27; "Concerning Differences," XXI, 567-71; "Old England," XXII (1900), 134-39; "Great Poetry," XXII, 278-82; "'T. E. B.,'" XXII, 424-27; "Brown the Poet," XXII, 582-87; "Pre-Raphaelite Brethren," XXV (1901), 257-63; "'R. L. S.,'" XXV, 505-14; "A Note on Slang," XXIX (1903), 136-39; "The Secret of Wordsworth," XXX (1903), 58-62.

PLAYS

IN COLLABORATION WITH ROBERT LOUIS STEVENSON

Deacon Brodie. Edinburgh, privately printed, 1880; revised edition, 1888.

Admiral Guinea. Edinburgh, privately printed, 1884.

Beau Austin. Edinburgh, privately printed, 1884.

Macaire. Edinburgh, privately printed, 1885; first published, New York, 1892; first published in England, *New Review*, XII (1895), 685-706.

Three Plays. 1892.

Four Plays. 1897.

EDITORIAL PROJECTS

London, weekly, Dec. (?), 1877–Mar. (?), 1879.

Millet's Etchings, with introduction. 1881.

Magazine of Art, monthly, Oct., 1881–Aug., 1886.

Scots Observer, weekly, Oct., 1888–Nov., 1890; continued as *National Observer*, Nov., 1890–Mar., 1894.

The Graphic Gallery of Shakespeare's Heroines. 1888.

Memorial Catalogue of the French and Dutch Loan Collection. Edinburgh, 1888.

A Century of Artists. Glasgow, 1889.

Sir Henry Raeburn, with monograph. Edinburgh, 1889.

Henley and John S. Farmer, *Slang and Its Analogues*, 7 vols. 1890-1904.

Lyra Heroica, with preface. 1892.

Tudor Translations, 32 vols. under Henley's direction. 1892-1903.

Henley and Charles Whibley, *A Book of English Prose.* 1894.

New Review, monthly, Jan., 1895–Mar. (?), 1898.

English Classics, 2 vols. only, *Congreve's Comedies, Johnson's Lives of the Poets.* 1895-1896.

A London Garland. 1895.

Henley and T. F. Henderson, *Poetry of Robert Burns*, 4 vols., with preface and Henley's "Essay." 1896-1897.

English Lyrics, Chaucer to Poe, with introduction. 1897.

Byron's Letters, Vol. I only, with essay, "Byron's World." 1897.

Henley and George Wyndham, *Poetry of Wilfrid Blunt*, with preface. 1898.

Works of Smollett, 12 vols., with introduction. 1899.

G. W. Steevens, *Things Seen*, with "Memoir" by Henley. Edinburgh, 1900.

Works of Shakespeare, Edinburgh Folio Edition, not completed. 1901-1903.

Complete Works of Henry Fielding, 16 vols., with essay. 1903.

BIOGRAPHICAL AND CRITICAL STUDIES
OF HENLEY

Andrews, C. E., and Percival, M. O., eds., *Poetry of the Nineties*, pp. 12-14. New York, 1926.

Archer, William, "Henley," *Pall Mall Magazine*, xxxi (1903), 125-30.

———, *Study and Stage*, pp. 61-67. 1899.

———, *The Theatrical 'World' of 1897*, pp. 319-27, 331-38. 1898.

Bailey, J. C., "The Poetry of William Ernest Henley," *Monthly Review*, xii (1903), 78-87.

Beerbohm, Max, *Around Theatres*, 2 vols., "A Puzzle in Literary Drama," i, 185-90. New York, 1930.

Benedetti, Anna, "*Un Poeta Inglese*," *Nuova Antologia*, ccxvi (1922), 243-48.

Blackburn, Vernon, "Henley," *Fortnightly Review*, lxxx (1903), 232.

Blackshaw, Randall, "Henley," *Critic*, xliii (1903), 261-63.

Boynton, H. W., "Henley's Literary Monument," *Dial*, xlv (1908), 453-54.

———, "W. E. Henley and Journalism," *Atlantic*, xcii (1903), 414.

Bronner, Milton, "William Ernest Henley, the Innovator," *Poet Lore*, xv (1904), 74-82.

Catalogue of the Library of W. E. Henley. 1904.

Chesterton, G. K., "W. E. Henley," *English Illustrated Magazine*, xxix (1903), 546-48.

———, "W. E. Henley—Poet," *Bibliophile*, i (1908), 3-6.

Cohen, Helen Louise, *Lyric Forms from France.* New York, 1922.

Cornford, Leslie Cope, *William Ernest Henley.* 1913.

Drinkwater, John, "William Ernest Henley," *Quarterly Review*, ccxxxvii (1922), 101-12.

217

Evans, B. Ifor, *English Poetry in the Later Nineteenth Century*, ch. XII. 1933.

Gilman, Lawrence, "The Achievement of Mr. Henley," *Independent*, LV (1903), 2038-39.

Greg, W. W., and Cornford, L. Cope, *Notes and Elucidations to Henley's Lyra Heroica*. 1900.

Hartley, L. Conrad, "William Ernest Henley," *Manchester Quarterly*, XXXIII (1914), 283-306.

Henderson, T. F., "Henley," *Dictionary of National Biography*, 2nd Supplement, pp. 242-46.

Hind, C. Lewis, *Authors and I*, pp. 130-35. New York, 1921.

Hoyt, Arthur S., *The Spiritual Message of Modern English Poetry*, esp. 185-208. New York, 1924.

Leroi, Paul, "William-Ernest Henley," *L'Art*, LXII (1903), 410-11.

Low, Sidney, "William Ernest Henley, Some Memories and Impressions," *Living Age*, CCXXXIX (1903), 150-58.

Lynd, Robert, "Henley the Vainglorious," *New Statesman*, XVI (1921), 507-8.

MacCarthy, Mary, *Handicaps*, "Henley," pp. 129-44. 1936.

Marriott-Watson, H. B., "Living Critics: I, William Ernest Henley," *Bookman*, II (1895), 186-88.

——, "Henley," *Athenaeum*, 1903², 92-93.

Masterman, C. F. G., *In Peril of Change*, "William Ernest Henley," pp. 39-44. New York, 1905.

Monkhouse, Allan, *Books and Plays*, "Three Plays by Mr. Stevenson and Mr. Henley," pp. 186-92. 1894.

Neff, Marietta, "The Place of Henley," *North American Review*, CCXI (1920), 555-63.

Nichols, W. B., "The Influence of Henley," *Poetry Review*, XII (1921), 153-59.

Niven, Frederick, "Henley," *Library Review*, XXVII (1933), 93-98.

Noyes, Alfred, *Some Aspects of Modern Poetry*, pp. 69-80. 1924.

Ould, Herman, "Henley," *Bookman*, LXXIX (1930), 41-42.

Parker, Gilbert, "The New Poetry and Mr. W. E. Henley," *Lippincott's Magazine*, LII (1893), 109-16.

Parrott, Thomas Marc, and Thorp, Willard, eds., *Poetry of the Transition*, note, pp. 345-47. New York, 1932.

Pennell, Elizabeth Robins, "William Ernest Henley, Lover

of the Art of Book-making," *Colophon* (1931), Part v, Section 9, pp. 1-12.

Runciman, Jas., "Charges of Plagiarism," *Athenaeum*, 1890[1], 403-4.

Schappes, Morris U., "William Ernest Henley's Principles of Criticism," *P.M.L.A.*, xlvi (1931), 1289-1301.

Shanks, Edward, *First Essays on Literature*, pp. 245-53. 1923.

Shaw, George Bernard, *Our Theatres in the Nineties*, 3 vols. 1932.

Shields, Roden, "A Blurred Memory of Childhood," *Cornhill*, NS xix (1905), 223-28.

Squire, J. C., *Books Reviewed*, pp. 95-103. New York, n.d.

Stephen, Herbert, "Henley as a Contemporary and an Editor," *London Mercury*, xiii (1926), 387-400.

Symons, Arthur, "The Decadent Movement in Literature," *Harper's New Monthly Magazine*, xxxvii (1893), 858-67.

——, "Mr. Henley's Poetry," *Fortnightly Review*, lviii (1892), 182-92.

——, "The Revival of Henley," *London Quarterly Review*, cxxxvii (1922), 16-22.

——, "Some Makers of Modern Verse," *Forum*, lxvi (1921), 476-88.

——, *Studies in Two Literatures*, pp. 186-203. 1897.

Thompson, Francis, "W. E. Henley," *Current Literature*, xxxv (1903), 364-65.

Watt, Francis, "The Portraits of the Henleys," *Art Journal*, 1906, pp. 32-38.

Whibley, Charles, note in T. H. Ward's *English Poets*, 5 vols., v, 498-501. New York, 1918.

Williamson, Kennedy, *W. E. Henley, A Memoir*. 1930.

Woods, Margaret L., "Poets of the Eighties," Walter De La Mare, ed., *The Eighteen-Eighties*, pp. 1-12. Cambridge (Eng.), 1930.

PART II

FRIENDS, CONTEMPORARIES, DISCIPLES

William Archer (1856-1924):
Charles Archer, *William Archer*. New Haven, 1931.

James Matthew Barrie (1860-1937):
—*The Greenwood Hat*. 1937.

J. A. Hammerton, *Barrie*. New York, 1929.

Denis Mackail, *The Story of J. M. B.* 1941.

James A. Roy, *James Matthew Barrie*. New York, 1938.

Wilfrid Scawen BLUNT (1840-1922):

—*My Diaries*, 2 vols. 1919.

Thomas Edward BROWN (1830-1897):

Sidney T. Irwin, ed., *Letters*, 2 vols. 1900.

Selwyn G. Simpson, *Thomas Edward Brown*. 1906.

Sidney COLVIN (1845-1927):

—*Memories and Notes of Persons and Places*. New York, 1921.

E. V. Lucas, *The Colvins and Their Friends*. New York, 1928.

Henry Austin DOBSON (1840-1921):

Alban Dobson, *Austin Dobson, Some Notes*. 1928.

Ford Madox (Hueffer) FORD (1873-1939):

—*Memories and Impressions*. New York, 1911.

Edmund GOSSE (1849-1928):

Evan Charteris, *The Life and Letters*. 1931.

Thomas HARDY (1840-1928):

Florence Emily Hardy, *The Life*, 2 vols. 1933.

Henry JAMES (1843-1916):

Percy Lubbock, ed., *The Letters*, 2 vols. New York, 1920.

Rudyard KIPLING (1865-1936):

—*Something of Myself*. 1934.

Joseph, Baron LISTER (1827-1912):

Hector Clare Cameron, *Reminiscences of Lister*. Glasgow, 1927.

William Watson Cheyne, *Lister and His Achievement*. 1925.

G. T. Wrench, *Lord Lister*. New York, [1913].

Sidney Low (1857-1932):

Desmond Chapman-Huston, *The Lost Historian*. 1936.

Will H. Low (1853-1932):

—*A Chronicle of Friendships*. New York, 1908.

Edward Verrall LUCAS (1868-1938):

—*Reading, Writing and Remembering*. 1932.

George MEREDITH (1828-1909):

—*Letters*, 2 vols. New York, 1913.

J. A. Hammerton, *George Meredith*. New York, 1909.

R. E. Sencourt, *The Life of George Meredith*. 1929.

Alice MEYNELL (1847-1922):
Viola Meynell, *Alice Meynell*. New York, 1929.
Anne K. Tuell, *Mrs. Meynell and Her Literary Generation*.
New York, 1925.
Coventry PATMORE (1823-1896):
Basil Champneys, ed., *Memoirs and Correspondence*, 2
vols. 1900.
Elizabeth Robins PENNELL (1855-1936):
—*The Life and Letters of Joseph Pennell* (1857-1926), 2
vols. Boston, 1929.
—*Nights*, esp. pp. 125-49. 1916.
Walter RALEIGH (1861-1922):
Lady Raleigh, ed., *The Letters*, 2 vols. 1928.
Auguste RODIN (1840-1917):
Victor Frisch and Joseph T. Shipley, *Auguste Rodin*. New
York, 1939.
Anne Leslie, *Rodin*. New York, 1937.
William ROTHENSTEIN (1872-1945):
—*Men and Memories*, 2 vols. New York, 1931.
William SHARP (1856-1905):
Elizabeth A. Sharp, *William Sharp: A Memoir*. 1920.
George Bernard SHAW (1856—):
Archibald Henderson, *George Bernard Shaw*. 1911.
Leslie STEPHEN (1832-1904):
Frederic William Maitland, *The Life and Letters*. 1906.
Robert Louis STEVENSON (1850-1894):
—*The Works*, 27 vols. New York, 1911-1912.
Graham Balfour, *The Life*, 2 vols. New York, 1901.
G. K. Chesterton, *Robert Louis Stevenson*. 1927.
Leslie Cope Cornford, *Robert Louis Stevenson*, with notes
by Henley, pp. 43, 49. Edinburgh, 1899.
George S. Hellman, *The True Stevenson*, esp. "The Hen-
ley Mystery," pp. 185-205. Boston, 1925.
Rosaline Masson, *The Life*. Edinburgh, 1923.
Alice D. Snyder, "Paradox and Antithesis in Stevenson's
Essays," *JEGP*, xix (1920), 540-59.
John A. Steuart, *Robert Louis Stevenson*, 2 vols. Boston,
1924.
William Wallace, "Scotland, Stevenson, and Mr. Henley,"
New Liberal Review, iii (1902), 79-86.

Katharine TYNAN (1861-1931):
—*Twenty-five Years.* 1913.
Theodore WATTS-DUNTON (1832-1914):
Thomas Hake and Arthur Compton-Rickett, *The Life and Letters,* 2 vols. 1916.
Arthur WAUGH (1866—):
—*One Man's Road.* 1931.
H. G. WELLS (1866—):
—*Experiment in Autobiography.* 1934.
Geoffrey West, *H. G. Wells.* 1930.
Charles WHIBLEY (1860-1930):
T. S. Eliot, *Selected Essays,* pp. 403-15. New York, 1932.
James McNeill WHISTLER (1834-1903):
Elizabeth Robins and Joseph Pennell, *The Life.* Philadelphia, 1919.
T. R. Way and G. R. Dennis, *The Art of James McNeill Whistler.* 1905.
Oscar Fingall O'Flahertie Wills WILDE (1856-1900):
—"Mr. Henley's Poems," *Woman's World,* II (1888), 108-12.
Lord Alfred Douglas, *Oscar Wilde.* 1940.
Stuart Mason, *Bibliography of Oscar Wilde.* 1914.
Vincent O'Sullivan, *Aspects of Wilde,* pp. 94-97. 1906.
George WYNDHAM (1863-1913):
J. W. Mackail and Guy Wyndham, *The Life and Letters,* 2 vols. N.d.
William Butler YEATS (1865-1939):
—*Autobiography.* New York, 1938.

PART III

LITERARY, SOCIAL, AND HISTORICAL BACKGROUNDS

Ashcroft, T., *English Art and English Society.* 1936.
Baring, Maurice, *The Puppet Show of Memory.* 1922.
Benson, E. F., *As We Were.* 1930.
———, *Final Edition.* New York, 1940.
Brie, Friedrich, *Imperialistische Strömungen in der englischen Literatur.* Halle a/S., 1928.
Buchan, John, *Memory Hold-the-Door.* 1940.

Burdett, Osbert, *The Beardsley Period*. New York, 1925.

Carré, J.-M., *Goethe en Angleterre*. Paris, 1920.

Chapman, Edward Mortimer, *English Literature in Account with Religion*. Boston, 1910.

Chesterton, G. K., *Autobiography*. New York, 1936.

———, *The Victorian Age in Literature*. New York, 1923.

Child, Ruth C., *The Aesthetic of Walter Pater*. New York, 1940.

Cruse, Amy, *After the Victorians*. 1938.

———, *The Victorians and Their Books*. 1935.

Ellis, Stewart M., *Mainly Victorian*. 1925.

Elton, Oliver, *C. E. Montague, A Memoir*. 1929.

Ensor, R. C. K., *England, 1870-1914*. Oxford, 1936.

Farmer, A. J., *Le mouvement esthétique et "décadent" en Angleterre*. Paris, 1931.

Harrold, Charles Frederick, *Carlyle and German Thought*. New Haven, 1934.

Hicks, Granville, *Figures of Transition*. New York, 1939.

Jackson, Holbrook, *The Eighteen Nineties*. 1913.

Kidd, Benjamin, *Social Evolution*. New York, 1894.

Lacon-Watson, F. H., *Lectures to Living Authors*. Boston, 1925.

Ladd, Henry, *The Victorian Morality of Art*. New York, 1932.

———, *With Eyes of the Past*. New York, 1928.

Le Gallienne, Richard, *The Romantic '90's*. New York, 1926.

McCabe, Joseph, *A Biographical Dictionary of Modern Rationalists*. 1920.

Manson, J. B., *The Tate Gallery*. 1940.

Marchand, Leslie A., *The Athenaeum: A Mirror of Victorian Culture*. Chapel Hill, N.C., 1941.

Moorman, Lewis J., *Tuberculosis and Genius*. Chicago, 1940.

Morley, John, *The Life of William Ewart Gladstone*, 3 vols. New York, 1903.

Murdock, W. G. B., *The Renaissance of the Nineties*. 1911.

O'Grady, Standish, *Toryism and the Tory Democracy*. 1886.

Petrie, Charles, *The Chamberlain Tradition*. 1938.

Rhys, Ernest, *Everyman Remembers*. New York, 1938.

Ross, John D., ed., *Henley and Burns*. 1901.

Saintsbury, George, *The Later Nineteenth Century*. Edinburgh, 1907.

Shorter, Clement K., *Victorian Literature*. New York, 1897.

223

Smith, Chard Powers, *Pattern and Variation in Poetry.* New York, 1932.

Sontag, Raymond James, *Germany and England: Background of Conflict, 1848-1894.* New York, 1938.

Stoll, Elmer Edgar, *Shakespeare and Other Masters.* Cambridge (Mass.), 1940.

Symon, James D., *The Press and Its Story.* 1914.

Vyver, Bertha, *Memoirs of Marie Corelli.* 1930.

Walker, Hugh, *The Literature of the Victorian Era.* Cambridge (Eng.), 1921.

Welby, T. Earle, *The Victorian Romantics.* 1929.

Williams, Harold, *Modern English Writers.* 1925.

Wilson, S. L., *The Theology of Modern Literature.* Edinburgh, 1899.

Wingfield-Stratford, Esmé, *The Victorian Sunset.* New York, 1932.

Woods, Maurice, *A History of the Tory Party.* 1924.

Woodward, E. L., *The Age of Reform.* Oxford, 1938.

Young, G. M., *Victorian England.* 1936.

225

Henley, Anthony Warton, 32, 73
Henley, Edward John ("Teddy"),
   32, 33, 89, 97, 100, 101, 101 n.,
   102, 200
Henley, Emma Morgan (mother),
   32, 33
Henley, Margaret Emma (daughter), 124, 153-54, 191-92, 194,
   198
Henley, Nigel, 32
Henley, William (father), 31-33,
   73
HENLEY, WILLIAM ERNEST:

LIFE

Birth, 31; ancestry and family, 31-33; boyhood, reading,
education, 34-38; first illness,
36; study under T. E. Brown,
39-40; Oxford examination, 40;
first operation and aftermath,
40-41; early verse, 41; treatment by Lister, 45; recording
of hospital experiences, 45-53;
visit from Leslie Stephen, 53;
meeting with R. L. S., 54; German lessons, 54; release from
hospital, 55; psychological effects of illness, 56-67; as journalist in Edinburgh, 71; meeting with Anna, 73; poverty,
73-74; editing of *London*, 74-
75; marriage, 74; as reviewer,
76-77; prose style, 72, 77-79;
first volume of verse, 93-95;
dramatic collaboration with R.
L. S., 96 f.; as literary agent for
R. L. S., 97-98; model for Long
John Silver, 99; at Nice, 100;
at "Skerryvore," 101; as art
critic, 111 f.; editing of *Magazine of Art*, 112-13, 121; visit
to Rodin, 121; quarrel with
R. L. S., 123-24; birth of Margaret, 124; political views, 127-
44; discovery of Kipling, 135;
editing of *National Observer*,
148 f.; estimates of his personality, 148-50; as talker, 150-
53; with Margaret, 153; as

editor, 154 f.; H. and Patmore,
156; articles on fashion, 158;
as literary critic, 162; compared with Ruskin, 174; with
Pater, 179; London verse, 183 f.;
growing reputation, 193; LL.D.
degree, 193; Margaret's death,
194; retirement from *N. O.*,
194; editing of *New Review*,
195-97; death of R. L. S., 195-
96; suggested for Edinburgh
Chair, 198; suggested as Poet
Laureate, 199; pension, 199;
death of "Teddy," 200; writing
of last poems, 201 f.; work on
Fielding edition, 205; first automobile ride, 206; last illness
and death, 208; Henley Memorial in St. Paul's, 209; posthumous reputation, 209-10;
compared to Dr. Johnson, 210-
11; estimate of his enduring
value, 211-12

OPINIONS

On art and dictatorship, 143;
art and life, 172; English romantic poets, 4; French realism, 157; French romantic era,
120; Regency period, 175; religion, 27, 65-66; reticence and
sentiment in literature, 156-57;
165; Toryism, 131; Victorianism, 164-65. *See also* aesthetes,
Arabian Nights, Arnold, Balzac,
Banville, Borrow, Boswell,
Brown, Burns, Byron, Champfleury, Chénier, Congreve, Constable, Corot, Delacroix, Dickens, Disraeli, Dobson, Dumas,
eighteenth century, Eliot, Fielding, Gladstone, Heine, Herrick,
Hugo, Keene, Kipling, Landor,
Lister, Meredith, Millet, Richardson, Rodin, C. Rossetti, D.
G. Rossetti, Ruskin, Scott,
Scribe, Shakespeare, Smollett,
Stevenson, Tennyson, Thackeray, Thomson, Tolstoi, Vanbrugh, Whistler